TRUE STORIES FROM NOVA SCOTIA'S PAST

TRUE STORIES FROM NOVA SCOTIA'S PAST

DIANNE MARSHALL

Formac Publishing Company Limited
Halifax

Formac Publishing Company Limited recognizes the support of the Province of Nova Scotia through the Department of Communities, Culture and Heritage. We are pleased to work in partnership with the Culture Division to develop and promote our culture resources for all Nova Scotians. We acknowledge the support of the Canada Council for the Arts which last year invested $24.3 million in writing and publishing throughout Canada. We acknowledge the financial support of the Government of Canada through the Canada Book Fund for our publishing activities.

NOVA SCOTIA   Canada   The Canada Council | Le Conseil des Arts
                                 for the Arts | du Canada

Cover design: Tyler Cleroux
Cover images: iStock Photography

Library and Archives Canada Cataloguing in Publication

Marshall, Dianne
       True stories from Nova Scotia's past / Dianne Marshall.

Issued also in electronic format.
ISBN 978-1-4595-0133-1

       1. Nova Scotia--History. 2.Nova Scotia--Anecdotes.
I. Title.

FC2311.8.M36 2012   971.6   C2012-903522-X

Formac Publishing Company Limited
5502 Atlantic Street
Halifax, Nova Scotia,
Canada B3H 1G4
www.formac.ca

Printed and bound in Canada.

PREFACE

Few places on the entire continent of North America can boast of such a colourful history as Nova Scotia.

As a child growing up in Halifax, I heard tales around our dinner table or in front of the fire on a winter evening, and I was hooked at an early age. It came as no surprise to family and friends, therefore, when I evolved into a bit of a storyteller myself.

A few years ago when I first began telling tales of our past in both the *Sunday Herald* and on CBC Radio's *Information Morning*, the response was, quite honestly, astonishing. It became clear, quickly, that the Nova Scotian appetite for good old yarns about shipwrecks, pirates, and even the occasional bloodcurdling murder was almost insatiable. And we do have a lot to choose from.

Many people go into the making of a book like this, not the least of which being the knowledgeable men and women who work at the Nova Scotia Public Archives, protecting our historic records for generations to come. At the *Sunday Herald*, I have had a wonderful editor in Paul O'Connell, who has a knack for finding just the right pictures to go along with a good tale. And at CBC, how fortunate I have been to work with people like Don Connolly, Louise Renault, and, of course, Margot Brunelle.

Margot and I began doing historic vignettes for CBC a few years ago and we enjoy every one. The stories in this book are some of our favourites, and I hope you enjoy them as much as we did.

CONTENTS

1

THE CARPENTER'S FRIENDS

(1752)

A widow loses her inheritance to the governor's friends.

In early 1749, carpenter John Aubony was a widower with a young son, living in Lyme Regis in the County of Dorset. Though he was a talented craftsman, work was scarce and Aubony was constantly on the alert for something that would provide him and his son some long-term security. One day, he found something he thought would be perfect. An advertisement placed by the Lords of Trade and Plantations in the *Sherborne Mercury,* and in most other newspapers across England, was calling for skilled carpenters to join an expedition to Nova Scotia. Free land and free food for a full year, with all the opportunities a new settlement could offer, seemed almost too good to be true.

In mid-April, leaving young Thomas in the care of his grandmother, Aubony was on his way to Portsmouth to sign on. It was a lot of work to ready the fleet for departure, but on May 14, along with dozens of other craftsmen, soldiers, and settlers, Aubony was on the deck of the *Winchelsea* as it made its way out of Portsmouth Harbour and into the great North Atlantic. He believed that, with hard work and determination, he would be well fixed in a few years' time and able to return to collect his son.

Six weeks later, sixteen vessels—Edward Cornwallis's ship, HMS *Sphinx*, followed by a hospital ship, a supply ship, and thirteen transports—dropped anchor at Chebucto Bay, and the harsh reality of a settler's life set in. Over the next few months, from dawn to dusk, the sound of trees being felled and buildings being erected echoed across the harbour. The backbreaking work, however, along with swarms of insects, the constant fear of Louisbourg-inspired attacks, and nothing in the way of warmth or comfort, took a toll. At the first opportunity, hundreds of settlers escaped aboard ships bound for the more civilized town of Boston.

As he had hoped, John Aubony's skills, along with determination and hard work, earned him a reputation among government officials as a master carpenter. There were dozens of other carpenters in the settlement but few had his business sense, and Aubony was often put in charge of the building of public works. As he and the Royal Engineers were kept busy erecting batteries, blockhouses, and palisades to hold off the enemy, Aubony's efforts were well rewarded and before the year was out he was on his way to prosperity.

During Halifax's first winter, illness brought on by the penetrating cold, poor diet, and a lack of sanitation claimed hundreds of lives. Aubony was a survivor, however, and by spring was more determined than ever to be a success. Before long, the small log huts along streets laid out in a grid by the Royal Engineers were being replaced by a variety of shops and more substantial houses. Soon, Aubony began to oversee the construction of his own home—one of several grand houses that lined Argyle Street, overlooking the Grand Parade. Not long after arriving at Halifax, Aubony had met a young woman named Dorothy Pickering and in early 1750 they were married. Within a year their first child, John, was christened at the newly constructed St. Paul's Church—a project that Aubony had also had a hand in. By early Halifax standards, John Aubony was a successful man.

With each passing day, Aubony grew more and more confident that he had made the right decision. His fortunes were growing, and, by 1751, he'd built and opened the Mermaid Tavern near the Naval Yard gate where he enjoyed the regular custom of men of the fleet. He felt fortunate in his choice of friends, as well. Robert Cowie, who owned a bakeshop just around the corner on Buckingham Street, was also growing rich, thanks to a recently secured contract to provide bread to the garrison. The two men applied for and received a grant of land that included an island in the Northwest Arm, where they set up a fishing operation. Soon, Aubony thought, he would return to England to fetch Thomas.

Another of Aubony's friends was Joshua Mauger, a distiller who had his hand in a number of other enterprises as well, including the slave trade. Of all the businessmen in town, Mauger was by far the most successful and the most ruthless. Though Aubony was aware that business in early Halifax wasn't for the faint of heart, he felt secure in his business dealings and his choice of friends.

But mortality rates, particularly for young children, were high in the mid-eighteenth century, and in April 1753 two-year-old John caught a severe chill and died. After an extended period of mourning, John Aubony realized that he had to make provisions for his family in the event of his own death and, on November 27, he drew up his will naming Dorothy, a second (as yet unborn) child, and his son Thomas as his principal heirs. As executors, he named his good friends Robert Cowie and Joshua Mauger and to them, Aubony left provision for the purchase of two mourning rings valued at one guinea each.

The following February, Dorothy gave birth to a second son,

also named John. Just months later, however, on July 3, 1754, the family was devastated once again when John Aubony, Esq., himself suddenly died. Among his bequests to Dorothy were their home on Argyle Street and the Mermaid Tavern. To Thomas he left his half share of the lucrative fishing operation on the Northwest Arm, having been assured that Robert Cowie would protect his son's interests until Thomas was of age.

Cowie and Mauger wasted little time. Within a day or so of the funeral they arrived at the door of Dorothy Aubony on Argyle Street and advised her that, contrary to what she thought, her husband had died in extreme debt and—they were sorry but—they would have to sell off his entire estate to cover those debts. And, strangely enough, he owed most of that debt to the two of them.

Dorothy didn't believe a word of it. John had always been a very careful man, and abhorred debt of any kind. She turned to the Governor's Council for help, rightly claiming that she and John's children were being cheated out of their inheritance. But she was a mere woman and, with no man to speak for her, she had no voice, not even in matters concerning her own family. As for Cowie and Mauger, they counted several members of the council among their friends.

At a tavern on the beach, they auctioned off or sold much of the Aubony estate, including the home on Argyle Street, and Robert Cowie became sole proprietor of the island in the Northwest Arm. Dorothy was left with only enough to rent a modest room in a house on one of the upper streets, and within months their second son followed his father to the grave.

While Dorothy lived in abject poverty, Cowie and Mauger continued to prosper. In 1759, Cowie was appointed to the council, and in the years that followed he and his second wife, Elizabeth, had several children. When Cowie died in May 1779, and the Governor's Council took the unusual step of securing

Cowie's estate until any claims could be determined, his sixteen-year-old son Robert became suspicious, and fought the move for almost two years.

On April 3, 1781, however, all of Cowie's property and possessions—including the bakeshop and the fishing operation on the Northwest Arm—were auctioned to pay off what the executor, John Butler, determined to be outstanding debts.

A businessman and a member of the House of Assembly, Butler was an unprincipled bully who would not hesitate to threaten or intimidate citizens, merchants, or government officials, and was not above lying to ruin reputations. There was one man, however, who had profound influence over him and for whom he would do almost anything—Joshua Mauger. Though Mauger had returned to England in 1760, through Butler he was still able to maintain considerable control over the business affairs of Halifax merchants. In the disposition of Cowie's estate, William Shaw, Mauger's attorney, was the auctioneer.

Like Dorothy Aubony, for the rest of their lives Robert Cowie and his brothers and sisters remained bitter over the loss of their father's wealth.

2

SEA MONSTERS

(1752–1853)

*Unlikely encounters with unexpected creatures
of the deep.*

Over the more than 250 years since Edward Cornwallis led the expedition of English settlers into Chebucto Bay, countless tales have stirred the imaginations of those who have lived along the shores of Halifax Harbour—tales of military might, horrendous tragedy, great celebration, ghostly encounters, and even buried treasure. Among the most interesting stories of all were those involving strange creatures of the sea.

In the 1750s, the French enemy at Louisbourg offered such a good price for English scalps that only the fearless or foolhardy ventured beyond the wooden palisades that enclosed the new settlement of Halifax. As a result, the harbour itself—which was filled with an abundance of fish and lobster—was especially important both as a means of recreation and as a food source.

On Saturday, May 27, 1752, while at the mouth of the harbour, local fishermen were startled by a strange creature entangled in their net. They hauled the carcass onto the deck and on the following Monday brought it into port, where they displayed it on the wharf for others to see. As word spread that a sea monster had been found, a curious crowd began to gather; over the next few days most of the town's inhabitants came to see it for themselves.

If drawings were made of the creature, they appear not to have stood the test of time, but the *Halifax Gazette*, on May 30, 1752, gave a clear description of it as a female:

> *…whose body was about the Bigness of that of a very large Ox, and something resembling one, cover'd with short Hair of a brownish Colour; the Skin near an Inch and an half thick, very loose and rough; the Neck thick and short, resembling that of a Bull; the Head very small in Proportion to the Body, and considerably like an Aligators; in the upper Jaw were two Teeth, of about 9 or 10 Inches long and crooking downwards, of considerable Bigness and Strength, suppos'd to be pure Ivory; the Legs very short and thick, including with Finns and Claws like those of a Sea Turtle; the Flesh and Inwards of this Creature upon being open'd appear to resemble those of an Ox or Horse, it has been shewn here for several Days past with satisfaction to the Spectators, and we hear the Fat of it is now drying up in order to make Oyl.*

By the turn of the nineteenth century, in a town with hundreds of taverns, brothels, and grog shops, sea monster sightings were generally thought to be hallucinations brought on by excessive drink and were rarely reported by Halifax's newspapers. But on the afternoon of Friday, July 15, 1825, a call on the offices of the *Novascotian* by a well-respected young gentleman of the town, who wished to remain anonymous—a man of "good family and excellent scientific education"—appeared to warrant further investigation.

At about three o'clock the previous afternoon, he said, he had been out for a ride in the company of a few young ladies, and, while passing Mr. Goreham's wharf on the Bedford Basin, noticed several members of the Goreham family and a number of their servants gathered on the wharf and along a nearby beach. They appeared to be watching something in the water. The young man and his companions stopped to see what was attracting all of the attention, and there, just a short distance off shore, they saw a large black object drifting on the surface. They tethered their horses and went to join the others at the wharf, though their curiosity turned to fright when the water churned slightly and the head of a strange-looking creature emerged and rose to about three feet above the surface. As it made no move toward them, the people remained very still and continued to watch. A full five minutes passed before the animal slipped beneath the water once again. In his view, the young man said, this was a sea serpent. It had no fins, and as it propelled itself forward the rest of the body followed with more than five or six large coils piercing the surface at intervals leading to the animal's tail. He described it as being as thick as a large log and estimated that it was about sixty feet in length.

Since the report had been made by the son of a prominent family, the editor of the *Novascotian* felt compelled to send a reporter to speak with Mr. Goreham, who was very obliging and not only confirmed the young man's account but also pointed out where the sighting had occurred. Goreham genuinely believed that what they had witnessed was indeed a sea serpent and as he was a respected member of the community, the editor of the newspaper had no reason to doubt his word.

Unbeknownst to the editor at the time, however, the serpent hadn't entirely left the area. About dusk on the same day another incident occurred several miles away in the waters south of Point Pleasant. Halifax resident William Barry and several companions were returning in a whaling boat after a few days in Prospect Bay. They were just below York Redoubt when Barry heard splashing nearby. He called out to the others that there was something dark in the water and it was approaching their boat.

Suddenly, as the men watched in horror, an enormous dark-coloured serpent drew near, its large, distinct head raised several feet above the surface. It began swimming around the boat, churning up the water and occasionally bumping into the sides as it went, terrifying the men, who could see the lights of houses in the distance but no hope of rescue. Occasionally, it drew back far enough for them to see at least eight coils of its body breaking the surface, causing them to estimate its length at sixty feet or more. Eventually, to their great relief, the serpent appeared to lose interest and headed toward the open ocean, taking off so quickly that it left a large, foamy trail in its wake. For several months thereafter, the sailors entertained locals and earned countless jugs of ale in exchange for their story.

A few years later, there was yet another occurrence. On May 1, 1833, ordinance keeper Henry Ince, along with four companions, set out from Halifax on a small yacht crewed by Jack Dowling, a retired navy man. They planned to do some fishing in Mahone Bay, about forty miles away, but at the halfway point they came upon a large school of grampuses (similar to dolphins) that appeared to be agitated. Some of the men picked up their guns and began firing at them for sport, when Dowling drew their attention to something else in the water.

At about a hundred yards away, they saw an object that startled them and in a later report they described the sighting this way:

...we saw the head and neck of some denizen of the deep, precisely like those of a common snake, in

the act of swimming, the head so far elevated and thrown forward by the curve of the neck as to enable us to see the water under and beyond it. The creature rapidly passed, leaving a regular wake, from the commencement of which, to the fore part, which was out of water, we judged its length to be about eighty feet; and this within rather than beyond the mark. …The head of the creature we set down at about six feet in length, and that portion of the neck which we saw, at the same; the extreme length, as before stated, as between eighty and one hundred feet. The neck in thickness equalled the bole of a moderate-sized tree. The head and neck of a dark brown or nearly black colour, streaked with white in irregular streaks. I do not recollect seeing any part of the body.

Such is the rough account of the sea-serpent, and all the party who saw it are still in the land of the living—Lyster in England, Malcolm in New South Wales with his regiment, and the remainder still vegetating in Halifax.

What Ince and his friends had seen near St. Margaret's Bay was the "80-foot long Petrel,"a serpent well-known to seafarers. Newspapers in Britain and North America frequently reported sightings along both coastlines.

It would be twenty years before another credible local sighting was reported. On Tuesday, August 2, 1853, businessman Peter McNab Jr., a resident of McNab's Island, was rowing across to Halifax about 6:30 a.m. when off the northwest coast of the island he encountered a strange creature moving rapidly with an *"undulating motion"* through the water, its head raised high above the surface. He reported in a letter to the British *Colonist* newspaper that he followed the animal for about thirty minutes until it finally disappeared at the far side of Georges Island. It resembled a large eel, he said, though its head was rather small in proportion to its twenty-foot-long body.

At the time, because of his position in the community, McNab's account was accepted as given. Twenty years later, however, he became violently insane and was committed to the Mount Hope Insane Asylum in Dartmouth. From that point on his story of the sea serpent was generally discounted as an early fit of madness.

However, just hours before McNab's experience, between midnight and one o'clock, there had been another sighting.

Captain Simeon Gates of Musquodoboit—a well-respected and sensible fellow—was on watch aboard his schooner just off the western side of McNab's Island when he heard the sound of a large animal in the water. It swam around the vessel, making a great splashing noise and blowing like a whale, for nearly three-quarters of an hour. Gates reported later that he had become increasingly concerned and was about to call out to one of the hands to pump bilge water at the monster to scare it away when the creature slipped beneath the surface and disappeared into the night.

As time passed, and ocean traffic increased, sightings became less frequent. But for believers sea monsters have simply moved further into the depths of the great North Atlantic, where they can avoid the two-legged creatures that live along the shore.

3

THE PUBLIC NUISANCE

(1758)

*Under the guise of charity, a house of horrors
on Spring Garden Road.*

In 1756, within a year of Governor Charles Lawrence's decision to drive Acadians out of the province, France had declared war on Britain at the start of what would be called the Seven Years' War in Europe and the French and Indian War in North America. Tensions between Louisbourg and Halifax escalated.

Inside the palisades that rimmed Halifax along Salter Street to the south, Buckingham Street (Scotia Square) to the north, and across the top of the hill, fewer than four thousand Haligonians were joined, whenever the fleet was in, by thousands of the king's fighting men. Overcrowding as well as unrestricted access to taverns and grog shops suddenly made the streets inside the barricades almost as dangerous as the forest outside, where Mi'kmaq and Acadian resistance fighters were lurking.

For some, however, these were prosperous times. Members of the wealthy upper class who lived in grand houses on Argyle and Hollis Streets were growing even richer from military contracts to supply and refit ships of war. Further up the hill, along the dingy lanes and courtyards that ran off Barracks Street, the business-minded lower classes ran grog shops and brothels from a collection of ramshackle hovels, eagerly pocketing the coin of the king's men.

However, along with prosperity came abject poverty. The poorest of the poor—widows, often with babes in arms, soldiers wounded so badly in the service of the king that they could no longer earn a living, the sick and elderly, as well as the insane—drifted about the streets in search of food, slept rough wherever they could, and, according to their betters, were a public nuisance.

Finally, in 1758, after receiving countless complaints, the Governor's Council acknowledged the need for a facility to care for the deserving poor, where they would work for their keep. Since Spring Garden Road, the principal land route out of Halifax, was on the outskirts of town and outside the south gate of the palisade, it seemed as good a place as any to locate the "unfortunates." There, near the corner of Grafton Street, on the original site of the main branch of the Halifax Regional Library, a large wooden house provided for the destitute well into the nineteenth century. In exchange for this generosity, some were employed as labourers on public works, while others (mostly women and children) were employed as little more than slaves in the grand houses of members of the poorhouse board of directors.

Life within the poorhouse was intended to be harsh, to deter anyone but the most desperate from applying for entry. And harsh it was. In its yard, stocks were erected for punishment of even minor infractions, and at a whipping post a keeper would make frequent attempts to beat the demons out of one poor lunatic or another.

These were society's unwanted souls and when they died

they were not welcome at St. Paul's Cemetery (The Old Burying Ground) as it was reserved for the more worthy of Halifax's citizens. Therefore, out of necessity, the land surrounding the building became the Poor House Cemetery. Residents of the place, however, weren't the only persons buried there. In the early days of Halifax, justice was harsh and executions fairly common. Many of the executed were carted off to the Poor House Cemetery for burial. In 1785 alone, twelve men and women were hanged, one fellow for no more than the theft of a few potatoes.

Many of the king's men were also laid to rest alongside the poor and the insane. After returning from battle during the American Revolution, for example, an entire regiment of Highlanders fell ill with a deadly fever. While their commanding officers were interred with ceremony under St. Paul's Church or in the church cemetery, the men were simply wrapped in shrouds and buried with haste among the "unfortunates." Several times a day, over two or three days, carts carried the dead from the military hospital to the Poor House Cemetery before returning for another load. There being no streetlights, the last load of the first day remained in an open grave overnight.

On the second morning, when a burial detail returned with more bodies, they were shocked to find a fellow sitting on the wall having a smoke—a discarded shroud lying nearby. The man had awakened in his grave in the middle of the night. It is believed that, though shaken by the experience, he eventually recovered from his illness and lived a long life.

Though Halifax was still considered one of the roughest towns in North America, by the 1790s things began to change. The royal influence of Prince Edward had given rise to what was struggling to become an elite society. (Edward, who would be crowned the Duke of Kent in 1799, and whose daughter would become Queen Victoria, had been ordered to Canada in 1791. He arrived in Halifax in 1794 and did not leave until 1800.) The palisades had disappeared, and wealthy merchants had begun to look beyond the town centre as a place to live and set their sights on Spring Garden Road and beyond. In 1805, thanks to the generosity of the prince, the governor himself moved into a grand mansion directly across from St. Paul's Cemetery. Among this new construction, the poor and the insane continued to occupy the corner of Spring Garden Road and Grafton Street.

Following the War of 1812, however, the need for additional jails was addressed in part by converting the poorhouse to a full-fledged Bridewell. The inmates were now joined by a collection of criminals. Petty thieves, pickpockets, and even violent rapists were thrown into the mix. Also included were children, sentenced to a month or more for stealing apples, or for sliding down a snow-covered hill (creating a traffic hazard)—unless, of course, their parents could afford to pay an exorbitant fine. On occasion the place served additional duty as a "dead house," where the bodies of murder victims were brought for examination and an inquest held.

By the 1830s, the poorhouse was dilapidated and living conditions were appalling. Drains from the place gave off noxious fumes, the food was often spoiled, and hygiene was not even a consideration. Abuse was rampant.

John Howe, the father of Joseph and a humanitarian of note, often visited the inmates of jails and prisons to give them what comfort he could. What he found at the poorhouse so offended him that he enlisted his son to take the matter to his colleagues at the House of Assembly. In a speech about the need to improve conditions at the facility, Joseph Howe recalled the evidence of his own father's eyes as to the cruelty of some of the keepers. One man, for some minor infraction, was forced to wear a spiked dog collar that pierced his bare neck. Another, a female resident, was placed in the stocks in the poorhouse yard for a full day and night, where she was subjected to the taunts and assaults of drunken men—for the offence of rejecting a keeper's affections.

The House of Assembly, however, did nothing.

The whipping post remained in regular use and several times a week folks strolling along Spring Garden Road were treated to the sight of a large black man named Hawkins wielding the whip with great enthusiasm. Hawkins was an escaped American slave who proudly wore the cast-off uniform of a York Ranger (green with red facing). He had found a new vocation in Halifax and took great pride in a job well done.

In sharp contrast, on land next to St. Paul's Cemetery (the site of the current courthouse) the governor commissioned a large, ornate garden where on summer afternoons the privileged class gathered to enjoy exotic plants and to listen to fine music from a bandstand. When the wind blew from the northwest, however, smells from the shallow graves across the way often caused well-dressed ladies to faint.

By 1867, a courthouse stood on the site of the Governor's Garden, the Bridewell had been made obsolete by the construction of Rockhead Prison at the north end of the city, and a new poorhouse had been built on South Street. As a result, pressure was brought to bear on the mayor and aldermen to provide "public space" for this area of town, and the now-unoccupied poorhouse grounds seemed an ideal location. The provincial government agreed to turn the land over to the city on the strict condition that it remain a public space in perpetuity and not be developed.

Well beyond repair, the building was demolished and park benches, a bandstand, and flowerbeds were installed. The Poor House Cemetery had become Grafton Park, and all reminders of what lay beneath the lawn were effectively removed. It soon became a popular spot for picnics, a playground for local children, and a place for gentlefolk to while away a summer afternoon. Within a few generations, memory of the Poor House Cemetery all but faded away.

In the twentieth century, when the municipal government was pressured to build a public library, they turned almost immediately to Grafton Park. The condition attached to the province's gift—that it remain public land—would not be violated, they believed, by the construction of a public building; and no thought was spared for the Poor House Cemetery. In death, as in life, the poor and the insane of early Halifax were of little consequence.

It appears, however, that some have never left. Since the construction of the Halifax Memorial Library in 1951, many visitors have reportedly encountered in the stacks a strange fellow dressed in the clothing of another era, who simply vanishes when approached. Others, who claim to have a gift for such things, have sensed an unearthly presence in every part of the property.

Since there are an estimated eight hundred forgotten graves beneath the library's lawn and the footpaths that so many Haligonians cross daily, perhaps it's not all that surprising.

4

DANCING IN THE STREETS

(1815)

Former enemies come together in celebration.

In the wake of the French Revolution in 1789, ongoing tensions between the two old enemies escalated until, on February 1, 1793, France formally declared war on Britain. A year later, numerous reported sightings of French ships patrolling the waters around Nova Scotia prompted the military commandant, Prince Edward, to invest heavily in the modernization of Halifax's fortresses and batteries.

Soon, Halifax became a depot for prisoners of war. As the first—brought from the West Indies—began showing signs of infectious disease, an old fishing operation on an island in the Northwest Arm was converted to a quarantine station. And, as the Royal Navy brought more and more captured French prizes into the harbour, the number of prisoners grew to such an extent that it became necessary to renovate the quarantine station to create a proper prison, complete with a hospital. The island was renamed for Britain's secretary of war, the Viscount Melville.

In 1811, while Halifax continued to be fully engaged in the war with Napoleon, another conflict was brewing in the mid-Atlantic. While ships from the Halifax Station were patrolling the east coast of North America watching for French warships, American merchants—to the consternation of the British Admiralty—were trading with all sides of the conflict in Europe, including Bonaparte's. To prevent the enemy from benefiting any further from American supplies, the Admiralty dispatched several heavily armed frigates from Halifax to help set up a blockade.

Relations between Britain and the United States, strained since the Revolutionary War, deteriorated. American anger at the blockade turned to outrage when the Royal Navy began boarding their ships and taking British-born crew members into custody, and worsened when several were charged with desertion and sentenced to death. On June 1, 1812, the United States declared war on Britain.

Within weeks, prisoners taken from American privateers and naval ships that had dared to engage British frigates were arriving at Halifax docks. Others were captured in Canada at battles such as Beaver Dam (June 1813) and Lundy's Lane (July 1814). By December 1813, the prison was operating at a higher capacity than ever before. Its cells and hulks contained more than twelve hundred American and several hundred French and Spanish prisoners, and the island guard had grown to its largest complement since the Admiralty first took ownership of the place.

The warders suddenly had another problem. The white Americans refused to mess with or to share the same sleeping space with the black prisoners—slaves who had gone to war alongside their masters. The French had no problem with the black prisoners, but seriously resented the white Americans. The language barrier added to the frustration. In no time, skirmishes were breaking out.

In the United States, newspaper reports on the treatment of American prisoners at Halifax were stirring up patriotic feelings.

On Saturday, November 20, 1813, for example, the *Niles Register* reported:

> *Melville Island where TWELVE HUNDRED Americans are confined is little above the surface of the water, and from its low situation is generally unhealthy—its circumference, about sixteen hundred feet—in this nauseous spot is situated a building that is two stories—130 feet in length and 40 broad—and of the upper room, 30 feet is set apart for the sick. The remainder of this apartment now contains 180 American prisoners. In the lower room are 770 more cooped up to breathe and generate disease by this narrow confine—350 more are near this island on board a prison ship. In this situation, under the most rigorous treatment, our brethren remain—the brave tars of our navy and many of the soldiers of our country are doomed to breathe their last from a pestilence which carries off three or four of a day—and to heighten the poignancy of their reflections, they are told by the British agent Miller "to die and be damned. The King has 150 acres of land to bury them."*

American newspapers, however, which regularly published accounts of troop movements and planned operations, also unwittingly hurt the United States' war effort by providing the British with that intelligence.

Meanwhile, in Halifax, the people were growing weary of both wars. Yes, through servicing the king's ships and the king's men, the economy was booming—but it had come at a heavy price. Mothers and fathers hid their sons from press gangs as best they could, and were devastated when their efforts failed. With the arrival of every ship, families waited on the docks for word of loved ones who had been pressed into service, and most often went away disappointed.

In the spring of 1814, there was a dramatic shift in the mood of most Haligonians, as word travelled rapidly across the province that Napoleon had abdicated and the allied forces had entered Paris.

A private soldier was dispatched to Melville Prison with an order that the French prisoners were to be released. After the Americans had been secured in their barracks, the French and Spanish were mustered in the prison yard for the last time and given the news.

While some of the French and their Spanish allies wasted little time in boarding the ferry for Halifax, others walked around the small island, inspecting it with the eyes of free men to see if it was indeed as horrible a place as they had believed. It was. For some, a visit to nearby Target Hill, the prison cemetery where old friends lay beneath the soil, was a must. After a few prayers and promises to take the stories of the dead home to their families, they too gathered up their belongings and headed for the ferry. As they passed by the barracks, some taunted the Americans—who could only watch from the windows with envy.

When they stepped off the ferry at the other side of the Arm, the men headed along a rough track that led toward town (Jubilee Road) and were invited to join Haligonians in celebrating the end of two decades of war.

Over several days, there were military reviews and salutes of the fleet, while merchants and other notables celebrated at the Exchange Coffee House and other establishments by feasting on hot suppers. At night, in a town without street lighting, a "grand illumination" was a sight to behold, when thousands of lit candles shone from windows that faced the street.

The first night, men, women, and children gathered around bonfires on the beach to watch fireworks displays from Georges

Island. Then a military band climbed onto the roof of the old market house, and the party really began. Hundreds came from all across the town to the old market place, filling the streets that fanned out from it—Hollis, George, Bedford Row, and Sackville. They danced, drank, and sang until the sun came up. And every night after that for more than a week, other bands took their turn on the market house roof and the party continued.

As happy as they were, most of the prisoners were most interested in getting back home and spent hours each day queuing up at the offices of shipping lines, hoping to find work on vessels departing for Europe. Others, however, had no desire to return to France after so many years, and welcomed the opportunity to take an oath of allegiance and remain in Nova Scotia. Many of these men found new homes among the Acadians.

Meanwhile, on Melville Island, the great bursts of light from the fireworks only served to remind the Americans of their situation and made their continued confinement even more unbearable. But their war would soon end as well. With the fall of Napoleon, Britain suddenly had seasoned troops at its disposal. Over the summer of 1814, large transports began arriving at Halifax, with thousands of experienced soldiers on board. They were dispatched to Quebec and across the British North American frontier, and in a matter of months the effort proved successful. On Christmas Eve 1814, emissaries of both Britain and the United States met in Ghent, Belgium, to sign the *Treaty of Peace and Amity between His Britannic Majesty and the United States of America*, which was ratified by the United States Senate in February 1815.

On March 22, the American prisoners left Melville Island as free men, to fully participate in a second celebration that, again, lasted for several days.

Britain's conflict with France resumed briefly in March, when Napoleon escaped and formed a new army. But after he and Wellington met on June 18 at Waterloo and word reached Halifax of Wellington's victory, there was once again cause for celebration. War-weary Halifax was in a festive mood.

5

MURDERERS IN THE RANKS

(1816)

*At Melville Island, not all villains were under
lock and key.*

As the wars with Napoleon and the War of 1812 seriously depleted
the ranks, Britain turned to the largest source of manpower it had
left—its prisons—and gave thousands of criminals a freedom of
sorts. In exchange for a lifetime of military service in the colonies,
and with the stipulation that they were never to return to Britain
or Ireland, large numbers of these men donned the king's uniform
and boarded ships bound for North America.

Before long, however, the new policy began to create havoc.
Many of the new recruits were rogues, who not only disrupted
operations but also committed serious crimes against civilians.
Although punishments for offences within the military were
harsh, crimes against townspeople were considered less important and usually resulted in no more than the soldier's being
transferred to another regiment. In a strange twist, some of these
former prisoners became guards at Melville Island Prison, both
during and after the War of 1812.

On the night of April 16, 1816, after the roll had been called and all was quiet in the soldiers' barracks, two such members of the guard—Charles Devret and Michael McGrath, of the 64th Regiment—slipped away from the island and made their way along the road to Halifax, heading for the Tremains' warehouse near the Citadel. When in town earlier in the day they had observed barrels of salted mackerel being carried into the building and had seen a way to make some easy money.

In his house on Barracks Street near the town clock, James Fleming operated a shop; it was known among the villains of the town that when goods were brought to him in the middle of the night he asked no questions. And so, when Devret and McGrath arrived with two large containers of fish between two and three o'clock in the morning, Fleming gave them a fair price for their "catch." After pocketing their money the two soldiers left, promising to return later with another load.

A short while later, Captain John Westmacott set out to do Grand Rounds on horseback. After being wounded three times in the Peninsula War while serving under Wellington himself, Westmacott had come to Halifax, still weakened by his wounds. He was an accomplished young man from a distinguished English family, and for most of his early years had aspired to become an architect. With the encouragement of his brother Richard—a noted sculptor and royal academician—John Westmacott did so well in his studies that he eventually won the Royal Academy Gold Medal for Architectural Design. When his education was complete, however, he chose to put duty before ambition and joined the Royal Army.

Westmacott was passing the town clock on the lower slope of Citadel Hill and starting down George Street toward the Grand Parade, when he came upon two men carrying large bags and acting suspiciously. At the sound of hoof beats the men dropped their loads and ran off in different directions, but Westmacott quickly overtook one of them. On horseback, he was an imposing figure, and soon had the man cowering against the wall of the Presbyterian Meeting House. Within seconds, however, the fellow's accomplice crept up behind the horse and, using a piece of wood, struck Westmacott hard enough to almost knock him to the ground. Before the captain could draw his sabre in self-defence, the first man pulled him from his horse; while Westmacott was on the ground the other fellow struck him several times with a cutlass and with his final blow declared, *"Damn him, we have done his business now…let us be off!"* and ran off in the direction of Barracks Street.

For several minutes Westmacott lay bleeding profusely from wounds to his head and neck. Though he managed to get to his feet, he did not have the strength to climb back onto his horse. In a desperate attempt to reach the fuel yard where he knew there would be men working, he staggered off, leaving a deep crimson stain on the snow behind him.

Near the Grand Parade he encountered a corporal's guard, who took one look at him and sounded the alarm. One of the men went in search of the medical officer, while the others carried Westmacott to his lodgings. He was able to describe his attackers as soldiers or men dressed partially as soldiers, though over the next seventeen days he drifted in and out of consciousness and said little more. At the attack site, investigators found the culprits' bags filled with salted mackerel, which they soon learned had been stolen from the nearby storehouse of Messrs. Tremain; in the snow outside the storehouse door was the distinct imprint of a cutlass. At about the time that Westmacott was being carried to his quarters, Devret and McGrath were on the road to Melville Island, where they arrived just before dawn and crept unnoticed into their cots.

On May 4, at the age of twenty-nine years, John Westmacott died of his injuries. The entire regiment, indeed all of Halifax, was outraged. As the general orders put it,

Headquarters, Halifax, 8 May 1816

The Commander of the Forces entertains no doubt that the troops in the Garrison fully participate in the feelings of horror and concern with which he views the inhuman and atrocious murder of Captain Westmacott of the Royal Staff Corps...

Most of the town turned out for Westmacott's funeral and lined the route between St. Paul's Church and the cemetery across from Government House. The inscription on his headstone reads:

> *To the Memory of*
> *Captain John Westmacott*
> *Of the Royal Staff Corps*
> *Died May 4th 1816 in the 29th Year of his Age*
> *His Death was occasioned by*
> *Wounds received from two*
> *Villains in possession of Stolen Goods*
> *Whom he attempted to Secure*
> *When he was performing Military*
> *Duty in Halifax early in the*
> *Morning of 17th April 1816*

Investigators were frustrated in their attempts to find his murderers, as in the weeks following the attack not one witness came forward. Therefore, on May 8, the commanding officer of the garrison announced that the government was offering a reward of one hundred British pounds for *"information leading to the Discovery of the Murderer or Murderers,"* and, as an added incentive to the troops, any soldier who came forward *"except the two men who committed the murder"* would receive a full and complete discharge from His Majesty's Service upon conviction of the murderers, *"if he so wishes."*

The magistrates and inhabitants of Halifax offered an additional £250.

Just days later, on the morning of May 11, an armed unit arrived at the gate of Melville Prison and took two members of the guard into custody. As other soldiers and hundreds of black refugees looked on, Michael McGrath and Charles Devret were placed in irons and taken away. The following day, while Devret and McGrath were appearing before the magistrates at the County Courthouse, a headline in the *Acadian Recorder* read:

"Murderers Caught!"

In determining whether there were sufficient grounds for trial, the magistrates heard from Mr. and Mrs. James Fleming of Barracks Street who, in consideration of the rewards offered, testified that between the hours of two and three o'clock on the morning of the attack, the two men had arrived at their house with about a half barrel's worth of mackerel. They set off to get more, promising to come back a few hours later, but returned much sooner than expected, empty-handed. Fleming testified that when he asked why they had returned without their bags, McGrath replied that they had *"met the Grand Rounds"* and had *"done his business…that he was dam'd saucy and deserved what he got."*

The magistrates bound them over for trial.

On Wednesday, July 10, at the Trinity Term of the Supreme Court of Nova Scotia, the attorney general, Richard John Uniacke, was adamant in his address to the jury that the crime was committed in cold blood with no thought other than the pleasure of taking a man's life, and that it was *"so atrocious as not to meet a parallel in military annals."* Soldiers and townspeople filled the courtroom, listening intently to every word of testimony. At the end of it, the jury took only ten minutes to return a verdict of *"guilty,"* and sentence was passed.

Despite Devret's continued claims of innocence in the murder, he and McGrath were given the same sentence and only a few days to contemplate their fate. On the following Monday, July 15, between ten in the morning and two in the afternoon, they were to face the hangman on the Halifax Commons.

In 1816, the Commons encompassed the area known today as the Wanderer's Grounds and it was in that general vicinity that military punishments and executions were often carried out. On the morning of the fifteenth, hundreds of spectators gathered near the scaffold to watch the killers of Captain John Westmacott get their just punishment. Also among the crowd were many who believed that an injustice was about to take place. It was clear to them that McGrath, the taller of the two—a sullen character if ever there was one—was the actual murderer, and that Devret's claims of innocence should have been believed. McGrath was the first to climb the scaffold steps. He was a tall and heavy-set man and when the wedge to the trap door was kicked away he fell instantly to his death. Soldiers standing nearby cut the rope and lowered the body into the waiting coffin.

As the hangman next placed Charles Devret over the trap door with the noose about his neck, he continued to cry and beg for mercy. Seconds later the trap door gave way and, to the amazement of everyone present, including Devret, he landed dazed but unhurt in the coffin lying below. Realizing where he was, he quickly jumped out. The rope had broken, and the onlookers were in a state of confusion. Blame was placed on the executioner, who many believed to be a woman in disguise, and a heated argument over Devret's fate ensued.

Most felt that divine providence had prevented the death of an innocent man, and expected him to be freed. Others believed no such thing, but felt that unless he was executed before two o'clock, as ordered by the court, he must be let go. As Devret waited anxiously with his priest and a guard, the argument continued. To settle the matter, a messenger was sent to Governor Sir John Coape Sherbrooke for a decision and most of the crowd left, expecting that Devret would be spared. Sherbrooke, however, was a harsh disciplinarian, and would hear no arguments in favour of the prisoner. He sent back this message: *"Tell the sheriff to get another rope and if that won't do, get a chain; he must be hanged."* Devret was executed at midday, with the same rope that had been used to hang McGrath. Both bodies were interred in unmarked graves on Camp Hill.

6

THE PRISONERS' REVENGE

(1805)

British justice and a secret society bent on vengeance.

Melville Island, presently the home of the Armdale Yacht Club, was for most of its history the site of a notorious prison and in the late eighteenth and early nineteenth centuries prisoners of the Napoleonic wars—French, Italian, and Spanish men among them—were confined behind its walls.

While their British captors had no qualms about meting out harsh punishments when required, the prisoners themselves had their own code of ethics, administered, sometimes brutally, by a clandestine group chosen by prisoners from among the most respected of their fellows and known as *le Grand Conseil*.

According to the diary of prisoner Francois Bourneuf (who settled in Nova Scotia after the war and went on to become a highly respected member of the Nova Scotia legislature) the most serious of offences were dealt with swiftly and harshly. In the case of a man who betrayed an escape attempt, for example, the offender was bound, gagged, and brought before *le Conseil*—at night, when the prison was quiet and they were less likely to be disturbed. By dawn the trial, conviction, and sentence had been carried out. Members of his own company had been required to stone the man to death.

In some instances, however, the Admiralty stepped in before *le Conseil* could act.

On April 3, 1805, prisoners taken from the French man-o-war *La Ville de Milan* were marched, as so many others had been before them, from the King's Wharf in Halifax along a dirt track across the peninsula and around the head of the Northwest Arm to the prison. Among them were two soldiers, Pierre Poulin and Jean Mari Quenie. Three weeks later, Quenie lay dead in the prison yard with Poulin's knife in his breast.

While some of the prisoners went to their fallen friend, others pounced on Poulin and, if not for the guards' quick action, he too would have been lying dead on the ground. For his own protection, Poulin was placed in the "black hole"—a damp underground cell, usually used to punish insubordinate prisoners. Waiting nervously for the escort that would take him to the County Jail in Halifax he could hear the commotion outside as the other prisoners loudly cursed and threatened him. It was several hours before they were brought under control and safely locked inside the barracks. Then Poulin was taken away in irons.

After being indicted by the grand jury before Chief Justice S. S. Blowers and Assistant Justices James Brenton and George Monk, Poulin was arraigned on the eleventh of July. His trial took place on the twelfth.

The Crown's only witnesses, Louis Mari Poisard and André Seamond, themselves prisoners of war, testified in English that the incident took place at lunchtime on April 26, when the prisoners had been sitting about the yard eating bowls of soup. Poulin, they said, had finished his meal and, setting his bowl aside, went into the barracks to retrieve his hammock, which he brought outside and proceeded to shake out. Quenie, seated on the ground nearby and still eating his soup, objected as bits of dirt were falling into the bowl. He told Poulin to move away. Poulin, however, refused and in response the other man said that *"unless you go further off, I shall get up and put you away."* Again, the witnesses claimed, Poulin refused.

In frustration, Quenie rose and, with both hands on Poulin's shoulders, moved him a step or two back. The witnesses hastened to add that this was done without violence or anger. Poulin, they said, still had the knife in his hand that he had used earlier to cut his bread, and swung at Quenie, stabbing him in or near the breast. Quenie cried out and fell dead to the ground.

The trial was conducted entirely in English. As Poulin understood only French, an interpreter—one of the prisoners of war who wanted him dead—was provided for him.

Before the justices and a jury of twelve, Poulin pled *"not guilty"* and claimed, through the interpreter, that he had reacted spontaneously to Quenie's touch when he spun toward him with the knife in his hand. He had not, he said, intended to kill him.

Poulin's court-appointed lawyer—who spoke no French—cross-examined the two French witnesses on Poulin's instructions, as indicated by the interpreter. There were no witnesses for the defence.

The jury, under the direction of Chief Justice Blowers, having found the witnesses compelling and M. Poulin's interpreted responses inadequate, determined him to be guilty of willful murder, rejecting the lesser option of manslaughter. A sentence of death was passed immediately and Poulin was led, in a state of shock, back to his cell.

Governor Wentworth, fearing that in wartime such an execution might send the wrong signal to the enemy about how they could treat their British prisoners, delayed setting a date of execution. On July 21 he wrote to London for guidance. The king and Lord Castlereagh, Britain's secretary of war (1804–1807), however, having no such qualms, left the responsibility firmly in Wentworth's hands.

Downing Street, London

…not having stated that any circumstances of Mitigation has occurred which might have induced His Majesty to extend his Royal Mercy to the Criminal, He has been pleased to command that under all the circumstances of the case, it should be left to your Judgement and discretion either to direct the sentence to be put in execution or to remit the same in such manner as you shall think most advisable.

Lord Castlereagh to Governor Wentworth, 5th September 1805

The governor and his council delayed making their decision for as long as they could but finally, on October 18, Poulin's fate was sealed.

Shortly after dawn on the morning of Thursday, October 24, 1805, the smell of chimney smoke was heavy in Halifax's cool fall air as spectators began gathering near the gallows site. At the County Jail, Pierre Poulin, after suffering through a sleepless night in the company of a priest, waited for the cell door to open. Shortly before ten o'clock a guard entered, placed him in irons, and escorted him and the priest to a waiting wagon.

With drummers leading the way, and an armed guard following close behind, the short, solemn procession made its way through the streets of Halifax to a place near the foot of the Citadel. Within the hour, Poulin's coffin was being lowered into an unmarked grave.

When the news reached Melville Island, his former shipmates believed that justice had at last been done.

7

THE HEROIC DOCTOR

(1809–1851)

A retired naval surgeon takes on the legislature.

Matthias Francis Hoffmann, a native of Trieste, Italy, joined the British Royal Navy as a young man. In 1809, while serving as ship's surgeon aboard the sixty-four-gun HMS *Inflexible*, he made his first visit to Halifax. There he fell in love with a local girl, Charlotte Mansfield. Though his ship set sail soon after, Hoffmann returned to Halifax in 1811 and, at his own request, was appointed naval surgeon to the prisoner-of-war camp on Melville Island. He and Charlotte were married in September of that year and eventually had six daughters and two sons.

When the Melville Prison closed in the spring of 1815 and the last of the French and American prisoners of war had been released, Hoffmann left the navy and opened a private medical practice on Granville Street near Province House. To further support his growing family, he took on whatever contracts he could, including one as surgeon to the 2nd Halifax Volunteer Artillery Company.

In 1827, an epidemic of typhus and smallpox struck Halifax and the legislature seemed reluctant to do anything about it.

Considering the town's long history with infected ships, this attitude was surprising to Halifax's small and overworked medical community. With the hospitals inadequately funded and equipped, the spread of disease could not be properly contained, and by the end of the year more than eight hundred had died. By 1831, the situation was so desperate that the magistrates, finally forced to take action, ordered the establishment of a lazaret (quarantine hospital). The logical place, they concluded, would be Melville Island—although its aging buildings were in an advanced state of neglect. With great reluctance, the legislature supported its refurbishment.

Matthias Hoffmann, Dr. Samuel Head, and Dr. John Stirling, all of whom had taken an active interest in the treatment of quarantined patients, were appointed to oversee the lazaret's operation, and in February of 1832 the legislature claimed some credit for a successful effort, reporting *"...the extension of the disease had been happily prevented."* Further, they established a health board under the direction of Dr. W. J. Almon to oversee health services across the province, and Matthias Hoffmann became a member.

Two years later, however, when Halifax was hit by an outbreak of cholera, the government ignored past experiences and once again stubbornly refused to fund the lazaret. By the time that epidemic was brought under control another four hundred lives had been lost. By 1839, Dr. Head and Dr. Almon had both died from typhus. Hoffmann succeeded Almon as health officer, but couldn't get the legislators to change their attitudes. While agreeing to provide a minimal amount of care for sick immigrants, they adamantly refused to allow the health board to quarantine infected ships from Britain, fearing a decline in trade. Halifax continued to be at risk from infected ships.

As health officer, Hoffmann faced an almost insurmountable task. Even Lieutenant Governor Sir John Harvey fought his efforts. Harvey was of the firm belief that if well-equipped hospitals were made available for the treatment of disease it would simply attract more contaminated immigrant ships to Halifax. And, when Hoffmann attempted to inspect cabin passengers on Cunard steamships, Samuel Cunard himself was able to convince Harvey that such scrutiny should be limited to the lower classes. Hoffmann was ordered to confine his inspections to steerage.

In May 1847, the barque *Mountaineer*, en route from Cork, Ireland, to New York, sought relief at Halifax. Typhus had struck in the crossing and many of its 279 passengers were ill. The arrival of so many sick at one time left the government with little choice but to open a lazaret in a small house in Richmond at the north end of Halifax. But the site was cold, damp, and impossible to keep clean. Because the townspeople were nervous about having the lazaret in their neighbourhood, Hoffmann was able to convince the government to allow its move to the old prison buildings on Melville Island.

While minimal funding was allocated for the purchase of medical supplies for the island hospital, Hoffman and his staff were faced with even more frustrations. The government refused to fund bedding, and patients who could not afford to buy their own did without. To make matters worse, fuel and food rations were in short supply and a guard was placed on the island to prevent any contact with Halifax.

Hoffmann and his assistant, James Hume, ran the lazaret until it closed in September. In its four months of operation, 203 patients were admitted, 10 were eventually discharged to the Waterloo Hospital for the Poor in Halifax, and 50 died. And Irish settlers who had set off with hope and anticipation of a new life in a new land were buried in the old prison graveyard.

Despite the dangers they faced and their many hours of devoted service, medical personnel in the mid-nineteenth century were poorly compensated. Hoffmann relied on fees paid by ships' captains for investigating illnesses on board and on contracts from the government to run facilities for contagious diseases. For his attendance to the sick from May to September 1847 at both the Richmond and Melville Island hospitals, for example, Hoffmann had to wait six months for a payment of £266. Hoffmann's income had never been enough to both care for his large family and prepare for old age, so he had little choice but to continue inspecting ships well past the time when most of his peers had retired.

Ships with suspected illness on board—other than those whose trade was important to the government—were required to moor in the stream, raise an orange flag, and wait for the medical officer to carry out an inspection. On one such visit Hoffmann was rowing past Georges Island toward a waiting ship when a rogue wave rocked his small boat and tossed him into the water. Two young soldiers from Fort Charlotte went to his rescue, brought him and the boat to the island, and gave him a hot drink and some warm, dry clothes. To their great astonishment, this elderly gentleman then thanked them sincerely, got back into his boat, and continued his journey to the possibly infected ship.

In late March 1851, the immigrant ship *Infanta* was bound for New York from Liverpool when illness forced the captain to put in to Halifax in search of relief. Within hours of its arrival, Hoffmann climbed aboard to carry out his inspection. It was, as suspected, typhus. A few days later, on April 3, 1851, Dr. Matthias Francis Hoffmann, seventy-one years old, became a victim of the contagion he had spent most of his life fighting.

The *Acadian Recorder* reported that such was the level of respect for him in Halifax that his burial at Camp Hill Cemetery on April 6 was attended, in addition to his wife and numerous children, by the town's most prominent medical men, by officers of HMS *Columbia*, and by a host of citizens.

8

SAVED FROM THE GALLOWS

(1839)

*A murderer…a lynch mob…and the startling
generosity of a young queen.*

On the west side of the Old Burying Ground is a stone that has
been a curiosity for several generations of visitors. It not only tells
how the occupant of that grave met his end, but it also names his
murderer.

It was 1839. The young Queen Victoria, who had been on the
British throne for just over a year, was being pressured to find a
suitable prince; France was celebrating Louis Daguerre's won-
drous new photographic invention; while for the troops, grog
sellers, and brothel keepers in Halifax, it was business as usual.

The wealthy merchant class, who had been in control of
civic affairs since the town's earliest days and who had grown
rich from the business of successive wars, now saw themselves
as gentry. They had graduated from their mansions on Argyle
Street onto grand estates in the suburbs, south of Spring Garden
Road. Along the east side of Citadel Hill, though, Barracks Street
and the rough lanes and courtyards that ran off it were teeming

with rowdies—both civilian and military—and any gentlemen or gentlewomen who dared venture there did so at their own risk.

Young James Bossom's story began and ended on Barracks Street, which, because of the frequency of drunken brawls, assaults, and murders that occurred there, was known among locals as "Knock 'em Down Street."

The Bossom family were fixtures in the neighbourhood, most notably because the patriarch, James Bossom Sr., was the innkeeper of the most notorious brothel in town, the Waterloo Tavern. For years, Halifax police had to contend with an almost constant stream of violent incidents there, and often Bossom himself was in the thick of it, happily cracking the heads of rowdies with the loaded stick he kept at his side. (A loaded stick was a shillelagh, a type of walking stick with the heavy end hollowed out and filled with lead or cement.)

His sons, from most accounts, followed in their father's footsteps. When he was barely into his teens, James Bossom Jr. was a sadistic young bully with a following of his own, a ragtag bunch of boys his own age and younger who had learned that whatever James wanted, James got—or else.

There were good families in the neighbourhood, of course, labourers whose meager wages left them with few other options and whose lives and the lives of their children were complicated by the likes of the Bossoms. So, on August 8, 1839, when at the age of twenty-three the young rogue came to an untimely end, feelings in some quarters of The Hill were understandably mixed.

About 6:25 a.m., young James Bossom left his parents' house and made his way to Clarke and Elexon's grog shop near the North Barracks Gate. He started pounding on the window and calling for Smith D. Clarke to come out and fight. For weeks now, Clarke had been refusing to give in to Bossom's repeated taunts of cowardice, even though on at least one occasion Bossom had assaulted Clarke and held him up for public ridicule.

The noise drew several patrons from nearby brothels and grog shops to the windows and many others spilled out onto the street. They were still feeling the effects of a night of debauchery, but they liked nothing better than a good fight, and this looked promising. Before long, a substantial crowd gathered.

In the days previous, Bossom had been bragging to his friends that he was going to call out this *"weak puppy"* and give him a sound thrashing. He stood his ground, and continued taunting and yelling until at last Clarke stepped out into the street waving two pistols. He hoped that by doing so he would frighten the rascal away. Bossom was not easily intimidated, however. With one hand thrust deep into a pocket, he moved toward Clarke, who became very agitated. Assuming he was about to be shot, Clarke fired twice, striking Bossom in the right eye. At the sound of gunfire, Clarke's business partner John Elexon rushed out of the shop to see what had happened.

Clarke, who was in a state of shock, stood staring at the guns in disbelief before dropping them to the ground. A sergeant of the 8th Regiment quickly took charge. He ordered two of his men to carry the dying young man to his father's house, and a sentry to take both Clarke and Elexon into custody and turn them over to the constables. Within minutes, word spread through the increasingly angry crowd that Bossom had not been carrying a gun.

In 1839, despite the obvious dangers of their job, Halifax police officers were unarmed and had no means of transportation; and so, as two constables took custody of Clarke and Elexon, a half dozen Barracks Street louts—still feeling the effects of a night of drinking—gave chase. The four men were forced to run for their lives down George Street to the large brick building at the foot of the hill that housed the police station, the courthouse, and City Hall.

Meanwhile, with James Jr. lying dead in the next room, an inquest convened that afternoon in the Bossom parlour, returning a verdict of willful murder against Smith D. Clarke and implicating Elexon for aiding and abetting. A mob quickly descended on their shop, smashing windows and stealing or destroying whatever they found. Both men remained in custody until their trial, as much for their own safety as anything else.

In the weeks and months that followed, tempers continued to run high along the upper streets. Rough friends and associates of the Bossoms regularly appeared outside the police station to vent their anger at the two men cowering inside. As a result, the trial was postponed until October and then again to the New Year, in the vain hope that tempers would eventually cool.

Early on Monday, January 20, 1840, Clarke and Elexon were led from the police cells to the courtroom above where the gallery was so filled with spectators that at one point during the trial there was fear that it might collapse. Outside, a mob of hundreds became more agitated as the day went on. The sheriff ordered all doors and windows locked and bolted, and put two constables at each entrance.

The entire trial, from jury selection to closing arguments, was completed in a single day and, after retreating for no more than a few minutes, the jury returned at 10 p.m. with their verdict. Elexon, a native of Shelburne, was acquitted. He left town immediately. Clarke, however, was found guilty, with a recommendation for mercy. Given the mood on the street, a messenger was sent to military headquarters and within the hour a contingent of heavily armed soldiers escorted Clarke past a jeering mob up George Street to Province House, where he was held under close guard in a basement cell. A few days later a sentence of death was pronounced. The execution was to take place in mid-April.

While much of Halifax society then turned its attention to the impending marriage of young Queen Victoria to Prince Albert, on The Hill excitement continued to build as Clarke's execution day neared. On April 1, however, the mail packet *Swift* arrived from London with a collection of royal dispatches for the governor, Sir Colin Campbell, including one that addressed the impending execution of Smith D. Clarke.

As an act of generosity, in celebration of the royal marriage, Queen Victoria had issued pardons to various felons across the empire, taking into consideration the evidence against them. Governor Campbell was surprised to find that one of the royal dispatches conveyed Her Majesty's gracious permission for him to reverse the sentence of death recently pronounced against Smith D. Clarke.

The mean streets of The Hill shook with anger.

Upon his eventual release Clarke quietly slipped away. Some said he went to Boston, to begin a new life. As for James Bossom Sr., he continued to run the Waterloo as before, and every now and then, when the subject arose, refused to be drawn into speculation that Clarke had never left Halifax at all and his bones were buried deep beneath a Barracks Street cellar.

9

A POOR, DEFENCELESS WOMAN

(1865)

Pulling the strings of City Hall.

For more than a century, business boomed in an area of Halifax known simply as "The Hill." Along the grimy streets, lanes, and courtyards that led off Barracks Street on the east side of the Citadel, row after row of brothels and alehouses did a roaring trade off the king's men and civilians alike. The innkeepers of these establishments were a rough breed who both employed and enslaved women of all sizes, shapes, and ages to work in their upper rooms, and were as familiar with the insides of the local jails as they were their own taprooms.

Despite fierce competition with one another, these denizens of The Hill had a code. When the police came to break up a brawl or to investigate one of the many assaults and murders that took place there, the brothel keepers closed ranks and did what they could to frustrate their efforts.

On September 20, 1865, many of The Hill's most notorious

citizens were sitting at the back of the City Criminal Court while one of their own was being tried for keeping a gambling and bawdy house. They watched as the prisoner was convicted and sentenced to six months imprisonment at hard labour. The gallery was filled to capacity and a cluster of curiosity seekers had gathered near the entrance—because the defendant was a woman!

In mid-nineteenth-century Halifax, few women ran any sort of business, and those that did generally confined themselves to dressmaking or to taking in laundry. Julia Donovan, on the other hand, had chosen to openly compete in a rough business dominated by ruthless men and, for her troubles, was now facing a stretch of hard labour at the new Rockhead Prison. Even so, she was a shrewd woman who already had a plan in place.

The very next day, on September 21, a petition was delivered from the County Jail to the office of the provincial secretary. A friend had drawn it up for Julia, who was unable to read or write. It asked for clemency and explained why she felt it was warranted. She was woman on her own, she said, who had been deserted by her husband three years earlier, and in order to make an *"honest livelihood to support herself and three small children"* she had been running a small shop. While some visitors to her house had, on occasion, acted in a disorderly manner, she claimed, there had been little she could do to prevent them, as she was just a poor, defenceless young woman. She begged to be allowed to return to the care of her children and said that, in exchange for clemency, she was willing to pay fines and post bonds for future good behaviour.

Witnesses to her signature mark (X) were Isaac Sallis, owner of the notorious Blue Bell Tavern near the town clock, and Thomas Murphy, who, as owner of the Waterloo Tavern on Barracks Street, was no stranger to riots, assaults, and murders.

Before deciding whether this petition was worthy of the consideration of Governor MacDonnell, however, the provincial secretary forwarded it to the mayor for his opinion. Mayor Mathew Richey, a Methodist minister, and Alderman Stephen Tobin, a successful merchant, quickly reviewed the petition, solicited the support of several colleagues, including Alderman Nash, and responded that same day. They believed, they said, that the sentence placed on Julia Donovan was far too harsh, and implied that the court must not have been aware of her family situation. As the governor was known to be a fair man, they hoped that he would agree to commute her sentence under the conditions noted in the petition and, further, they said they would each guarantee bonds for her good behaviour.

When the file landed on Governor MacDonnell's desk, he replied within days:

> *The only thing approaching to a possible change in the judgment…appears to be the position of the convict's family; that, however, is quite beside the merits of this case. If any change be made in the sentence it should, therefore, be a change which would maintain, as far as possible, the severity of the present sentence, and I do not think any fine less than $100 would prevent the appearance of undue partiality.*

He agreed to the terms suggested by the petition and guaranteed by the mayor and Alderman Tobin. Within days of her conviction, Julia Donovan was fined one hundred dollars, which was equivalent to a factory worker's annual wage, and released under bonds for good behaviour.

Fortunately for Julia, her friends at City Hall had neglected to inform the governor that she was no stranger to Rockhead Prison, having spent ten days there the previous July for public drunkenness.

Julia had been out of jail for about a week when, on October 2, the citizens of Halifax turned out for a civic election. Doing their part, Isaac Sallis, Thomas Murphy, and Julia herself openly encouraged their customers to support those members of the City Council who had contributed to her release. The fact that most of the voters in town passed through The Hill establishments at one time or another had not been lost on her City Hall supporters.

With Mayor Richey, Alderman Tobin, and Alderman Nash easily re-elected, several prominent commentators weighed in to link their successes to the men's support for the concept of Canadian confederation. Jonathan McCully, for example, a recent convert to the concept, claimed in a letter to the *Times of London* that the election and re-election of the best Halifax had to offer (all members of the Pro-Confederation Party) was, in fact, a result of the excitement attending talk of having Nova Scotia become a part of Canada.

Well after the election, the *British Colonist* and *Acadian Recorder* newspapers began fresh reporting on the Julia Donovan affair, after receiving a number of tips from anonymous sources at City Hall. With every report, more people began asking questions. Julia Donovan became the talk of the town. Even in the finer drawing rooms of Halifax, where the conversation would never willingly turn to the goings-on of The Hill, people were expressing outrage over the influence that these dens of iniquity appeared to have over the Halifax City Council.

Newspapers as far away as Charlottetown and St. John's began picking up the story, and, before long, Julia was being credited with the outcome of the Halifax civic election. Ridicule was heaped on all of those who had claimed victory for the Pro-Confederation Party. The *Charlottetown Patriot* said:

"An Obvious Interfence"

...Aldermen and would-be mayors would fain secure their ends by the aid of Julia and her peers! Is Julia one of the "leading" minds of the Lower Provinces?

Most of Halifax was outraged. Julia Donovan was well known about the town, people claimed, so ignorance of her reputation was no excuse. She was a rowdy brute of a woman who had her own sister—Jane Scanlan—working in her brothel. People were not surprised to learn the names of her supporters who were in the same line of work, and who, thanks to the sheer numbers of men who regularly crossed their thresholds, were known to have considerable political influence.

Aldermen suddenly found themselves being accosted in the street by citizens demanding an explanation. There was so much anger being directed at the entire city council, in fact, that—over the objections of the mayor and a few others who had participated in her release—a committee was struck to look into the matter.

In November the investigating committee spent several weeks reviewing the provincial secretary's file and taking depositions from everyone involved. One of the key witnesses, however, was no longer available. Governor MacDonnell had left Halifax soon after Julia's release and was now governor of Hong Kong. His replacement, Governor Hastings Doyle, had absolutely no knowledge of the matter.

The depositions were an outrage in themselves.

Julia's sister, Jane Scanlan, was deposed. She had no hesitation in admitting that Alderman Stephen Tobin had given her a guarantee that he would personally ensure Julia's release—provided that she (Jane) would agree to speak with the other brothel keepers on The Hill to solicit their support for himself and for a number of his colleagues during the coming civic election. Jane told the committee that she had been happy to do so.

Isaac Sallis was fairly blatant about the power he wielded at City Hall, and didn't require prompting from Jane Scanlan to get involved in the election campaign, as he had already reached an agreement with some of his "many friends" there. He told the committee that his election activity had been a direct result of

Julia Donovan's release. Sallis claimed that his influence extended to several aldermen, including Tobin and Nash, both of whom had approached him for support.

When the committee appeared before the Council in December at a public meeting, their report was openly discussed and many of the documents were read aloud. All documentation was then filed away.

Later, when they went in search of the entire file on the matter, the newspaper editors who had been following the story with great enthusiasm were disappointed, but not entirely surprised, to find that the file containing the relevant correspondence, depositions, and Julia's petition had mysteriously disappeared.

Not one person was punished, and the election results were allowed to stand.

10
ESCAPE OF THE SOUTHERN PIRATE

(1863)

The American Civil War on a Halifax wharf.

At the outbreak of the U.S. Civil War in 1861, the sympathies of most Haligonians were quite naturally with their northern friends. Bostonians had helped to build Halifax in 1749, and since then, ongoing trade between Nova Scotia and New England had created a strong bond. However, as the war progressed and more lucrative trade opportunities opened up with the Confederate States, things began to change. Though the concept of slavery was abhorrent to most of Halifax, the town's wealthy business class readily embraced the southern cause.

Since warships from both sides used Halifax to refit and supply, Northern and Southern agents took up residence and staked out their respective territories in the town's hotels and inns. Newspapers openly supported one side or another and, much to the chagrin of the U.S. Consul M. M. Jackson, Confederate officers en route to and from Canada or Europe were generously hosted by some of the town's most prosperous citizens.

In the early hours of December 8, 1863, an act of piracy brought the war even closer.

Sixteen passengers who boarded the steamer *Chesapeake* at New York were actually Confederates in disguise, and before the ship could reach its destination of Portland, Maine, they struck. In the struggle to gain control of the ship, the pirates, led by John C. Braine, shot and killed the second engineer, Orin Schaffer, and seriously wounded two others. After Schaffer's body had been tossed overboard, Captain Willett and all but a few crew members were ordered into a small boat and the *Chesapeake* set an easterly course toward Nova Scotia.

When the small boat finally reached St. John, New Brunswick, Willett raised the alarm and a number of unarmed American vessels were soon tracking the *Chesapeake's* progress along the coast of Nova Scotia.

One of the pirates knew these waters well. Vernon Locke, a native of Shelburne, took over as captain and on December 16 moored the ship near Sambro. He and a landing party set off on foot for Halifax, returning much later with a schooner-load of coal and two newly hired engineers.

Just before daybreak on December 17, Lieutenant John Nichols, commanding officer of an armed U.S. steamer, the *Ella and Annie*, came upon the *Chesapeake* while it was taking on the coal. At the sight of the steamer bearing down on them, the pirates climbed into a small boat and headed for shore, where they ran into the woods and out of sight. Only one remained behind. George Wade, a well-known villain who had spent time in Sing Sing Prison for armed robbery, was found sleeping in his bunk. The two newly hired Scottish engineers, brothers William and Alexander Henry, were also taken into custody.

Though Lieutenant Nichols would have preferred to return to the United States, he was in British waters and bound by law to take his prize into Halifax. With the *Chesapeake* in tow and in the company of the gunship USS *Dacotah*, the *Ella and Annie* arrived at Halifax that afternoon and, with its prisoners in irons, remained moored in the stream until the afternoon of Saturday, the nineteenth.

On Sheriff J. J. Sawyer's recommendation, word was sent to the American ship that the prisoners were to be brought ashore at the Queen's Wharf where the Henry brothers would be formally released and George Wade arrested on charges of piracy and murder on the high seas.

The lieutenant governor was away at the time and in his absence the administration of Nova Scotia fell to the senior military officer of the day, Sir Charles Hastings Doyle, for whom security was a major concern. Doyle ordered that access to the wharf be restricted to *"respectably dressed citizens."* His theory that only the poorly dressed presented a problem, however, was about to be tested.

As the small boat bearing the prisoners came in, Sheriff Sawyer stood closest to the slip, while City Marshal Garrett Cotter, Police Sergeant Lewis Hutt, and two constables stood a few feet away. Though it was unusual for a Halifax police officer to be armed, tensions were running so high that, as a precaution, a pistol had been assigned to Sergeant Hutt. As the small boat reached the slip, close to a hundred spectators that stood behind the police became increasingly agitated and newspapers later reported that these respectable citizens, so trusted by the authorities, behaved no differently from any other boisterous mob—even poorly dressed ones. Onlookers lined the decks of nearby vessels and a whaler moved close to the dock, its two occupants watching the goings-on with some interest.

The prisoners were escorted up the slip in shackles, with George Wade—a thin, rough-looking fellow with a shaggy, yellowish-gray beard—bringing up the rear. Just as the sheriff finished reading a document to release the Henry brothers from custody, the shackles of all three were removed. From the crowd of spectators, Dr. William J. Almon stepped forward and, as if taking their cue from him, several others moved quickly to put themselves between him and the policemen. Suddenly, Almon grabbed Wade's arm and rushed him to a gangplank leading to the whaler below.

Sergeant Hutt, who managed to push his way through the mob, reached for his pistol and called out, *"Stop, in the name of the queen!"* Before he could fire a warning shot into the air, however, Alexander Keith Jr. wrested the gun from his hand, while Almon and another spectator, Dr. Peleg Smith, each grabbed one of Hutt's arms.

If ever there was an indication of Southern support in Halifax, this was it. Respectably dressed citizens entirely surrounded the police officers and prevented them from doing anything to stop the escape, while cheering and shouting for Wade to get away. Wade was so bold that as the boat moved away from the dock he shouted, *"For God's sake, thank the queen for my liberty!"*

The police were further frustrated by the lack of a boat, and by the terms of the arrest warrant, which limited their authority to the town of Halifax, effectively preventing them from pursuing Wade.

When the crowd finally dispersed, three well-connected men of the community were arrested for "interfering with the police in the discharge of their duty." Dr. Almon was of a long line of highly respected Halifax physicians and a professor at the Dalhousie Medical College, Dr. Smith was another well-known physician, and Alexander Keith Jr. was the nephew of a successful brewer who sat as a member of the legislature.

In January, Sir Charles Hastings Doyle presided over a hearing, the outcome of which would undoubtedly have diplomatic repercussions. Confederate sympathizers in Halifax, as well as the U.S. government, were paying close attention and he had to find a way to appease both sides.

He did.

Almon, Smith and Keith claimed that by drawing his gun, Hutt—one of the most admired officers on the force—had acted recklessly and without care of the innocent people around him. They stepped in, they claimed, only to protect bystanders. This seemed good enough for Doyle, who simply wanted the matter concluded with as little fuss as possible. He acquitted the three on the grounds that they had acted in the best interests of the public.

Though the subject of some speculation among supporters of the North, the incident on the Queen's Wharf had no lasting impact on the Haligonians involved. Hastings Doyle went on to become lieutenant governor; Dr. William J. Almon was elected in 1872 as a Conservative member of the legislature; Dr. Smith continued to enjoy a prosperous life; and Keith remained a Confederate agent until the end of the war.

Though it was a frustrating exercise for them, the fine reputations of both Marshal Cotter and Sergeant Hutt remained intact and, in time, Cotter became Halifax's first chief of police and Hutt was promoted to detective.

As for the pirates, only three—all British born—were detained in New Brunswick on an American extradition warrant. Rather than risk antagonizing both the Confederacy and Britain in favouring the U.S. government, Judge Thomas Ritchie decided that as the act of piracy had not occurred in the territorial waters of the United States, the warrant was invalid, and the men were released.

Interestingly, Judge Ritchie was also the brother-in-law of Dr. William J. Almon.

In all of this, the murder of Orin Schaffer aboard the *Chesapeake* steamer was largely forgotten.

11

THE SOLDIERS' RIOT

(1863)

Hundreds of redcoats lay siege to Halifax.

A staunchly British town, nineteenth-century Halifax rarely missed an opportunity to commemorate important events in the lives of its royal family, and at daybreak on Tuesday, April 14, 1863, its streets were dressed to perfection for a grand celebration.

In the early morning light, the Volunteer Artillery, accompanied by the Royal Artillery Band, kicked off the celebrations with a rousing salute. The town was suitably dressed for the occasion—to honour the royal wedding of Prince Edward Albert to Princess Alexandra of Denmark, which had taken place on March 10 at Windsor Castle. Every public building, private residence, and street lamp was flying the Union Jack and trimmed with bunting and silks bearing the royal colours, the plumes of the Prince of Wales, and bridal wreaths of all sizes and descriptions.

Beginning at 10 a.m., companies of volunteers and regulars, with their respective bands, gathered at the Grand Parade and from there the grand marshal led a procession through the streets. Bright sunlight bounced off polished bayonets and bands competed for the attention of onlookers gathered along the sidewalks and rooftops of Argyle, Brunswick, Jacob, George, Barrington, and Hollis Streets, stirring up patriotic feelings before returning to the Grand Parade.

At noon, the Royal Artillery conducted another salute from the Citadel and, shortly after, attention turned once again to the Grand Parade where soldiers were to participate in sporting events. The lieutenant governor and his wife, the Earl and Countess of Mulgrave, took their places on the steps of Dalhousie College (on the site of the present City Hall) and the games began. So many townspeople surrounded the square to watch that several events had to be cancelled because there was simply not enough room to hold them, and a number of small trees along Argyle Street fell under the weight of spectators who had climbed them to get a better view.

That evening, after attending a torchlight parade, some of the more genteel folk of the town went on to a formal dinner at the Halifax Hotel, and rounded out the festivities with a grand ball at the Masonic Hall. Just a short walk away, soldiers of the garrison and the town's rowdiest inhabitants were roaming the brothels and groggeries that lined the dingy streets near the Citadel. Soon, the festive atmosphere took on a darker tone.

At the notorious Blue Bell Tavern at the top of George Street near the town clock, Daniel McCarthy, a soldier who had been drinking in the taproom for several hours, was ordered to leave after he hit a woman with his fist. When he refused, tavern keeper Michael Hines put him out by force. Now, it was the general consensus within the ranks that Haligonians did not respect them and often sought to embarrass or humiliate them. So, when the ousted soldier told his friends his version of what had happened, dozens of angry men returned with him to the Blue Bell. They rushed en masse into the house, confronted Hines, and forced him back against the wall near the staircase where Mrs.

Hines handed her husband a "loaded stick" with which to defend himself.

As word of the altercation spread, a horde of civilian ruffians rushed in and an all-out brawl followed, with dozens of angry men brandishing sticks, belts, and slingshots. It took almost three hours for city constables and a military patrol to get things under control. At the end of it, Daniel McCarthy was bleeding profusely from a head wound and Michael Hines was in custody for assaulting him. While the remaining soldiers were rounded up and returned to barracks, their civilian opponents ran off in several directions.

The next day, tempers were still running high. Close to a dozen soldiers of the 17th set off for Barracks Street where they attacked another brothel, the Waterloo Tavern, and tried unsuccessfully to set it alight before moving on to Brunswick, Creighton, and Gottingen Streets, smashing windows of shops and homes and beating senseless any unfortunate civilian they happened to come upon.

Two consecutive days of rowdyism were enough for the city authorities, and on Thursday morning several special constables were sworn in to supplement the police force. About six o'clock that evening, however, the real trouble began.

Swarms of soldiers converged on Barracks Street, determined to settle scores with civilians for every conceivable slight, and soon three hundred drunken redcoats from the 16th and 17th Regiments were gathered near the town clock. Once the signal was given, the entire mass rushed together down George Street yelling as loudly as they could, wielding sticks, stones, slingshots, and belts with the buckles turned out. Any civilian caught in their path was pushed to the ground and pummelled. With a soldier carrying a white flag in the lead, the mob continued on through the Grand Parade and down George Street to Hollis, shouting obscenities and threats along the way. The sound was deafening to the occupants of buildings along the route, who looked out with fear, then drew shutters and locked their doors.

No one near the mob was safe, and when they came upon Captain O'Brien of the packet *Halifax* in front of Province House, they beat him within an inch of his life. At the corner of Prince the mob made a right turn and raced back up toward Barrington, then headed once more for George and down the hill again, this time to the bottom where a building housing the court house, police station, and city hall stood on the northwest corner of Water Street. Arming themselves with stones from a nearby ditch, the great throng pelted the doors and windows of City Hall until no pane of glass remained intact and the lantern at its entrance was smashed beyond repair.

A handful of special constables and members of the police night watch held the crowd back and paid the price with broken arms and skulls. A policeman, John Sheehan, was badly hurt. Inside, aldermen and court officials bolted and barred the doors and windows, while, at the Water Street side of the building, at the entrance to the police station, the same thing was going on. A woman trying to cross George Street to get to the safety of her own home was chased down by a soldier and severely beaten about the head with his belt.

After having inflicted as much damage as possible, the mob regrouped and rushed back up George Street, screaming and shouting as they went. By this time all of the shops and offices along the route were closed. Fearing the worst, the occupants had set off for the relative safety of their homes while the redcoats had been otherwise engaged at the foot of the hill. The noise could be heard more than a mile away, and became even greater when the fire department turned on its alarm to call volunteers to the scene. At the corner of George and Barrington the soldiers stopped and made a stand, as another mob—of hundreds of civilian thugs— had formed and, brandishing bludgeons of all shapes and sizes, was gathering steam on the Grand Parade. Though the governor, several members of the House of Assembly, civic dignitaries, and volunteer firemen tried to quell the disturbance, stones were flying from all directions. There was little they could do.

Two companies of engineers and several lines of piquets with bayonets affixed were dispatched to restore order. At the sight of them, the civilian thugs scattered. The soldiers rushed back up to the top of George Street. There, commanding officers tried to convince them to give up and return to barracks, only to be spat upon and jeered.

A company of the Royal Artillery was called out. They managed to secure about half of the rioters at gunpoint, and escorted about a hundred to the Citadel and fifty others to their barracks. In the confusion, the remaining 150 set off in several directions. When, about eight o'clock, things finally became quiet, it was an uneasy peace. Piquets were stationed at major thoroughfares all night while armed police and special constables patrolled the streets. Gradually, dozens of red-coated louts emerged from their hiding places and headed for Spring Garden Road, where they began to indiscriminately smash shop windows and attack innocent bystanders. Then civilian ruffians arrived and the brawl resumed. Before it could be brought under control by the Royal Artillery, a large number of men were nursing cuts and bruises and a badly injured soldier of the 17th Regiment had been carried off to the military hospital. The arrested redcoats were confined to the Citadel and the ringleaders of the civilian gangs were locked in cells at the police station.

On Friday, April 17, just when they thought it was safe to leave their houses again, Haligonians were thrown into another state of panic and began arming themselves as word spread that soldiers had attacked another civilian. At three o'clock, on his way into the city from the Richmond Railway Depot, an engine driver, George Clelland, had been brutally assaulted.

In the days that followed, the town was relatively quiet, and on Tuesday, April 21, to ensure it remained so, 120 special constables were sworn in at the police court for a period of fourteen days. Special constables were chosen from the business community, and though most resented being called to duty there was a hefty fine for refusing—eight dollars. On April 24, after a week's confinement, soldiers who had participated in the riot were returned to duty, and extra patrols were laid on to prevent any further problems.

Several trials stemmed from the violence of April 14 to 18. Michael Hines, the proprietor of the Blue Bell Tavern, was tried before the Supreme Court, found guilty of assault, sentenced to four months at hard labour at Rockhead Prison, and fined eighty dollars. The soldiers who attacked George Clelland were sentenced to several months at hard labour at the Melville Island Prison.

There was no justice for John Sheehan, however. The forty-year-old policeman died of his injuries on June 9, leaving a wife and several children. On Wednesday, June 14, City Council approved two hundred dollars in compensation to his widow.

In the 1860s there were more than three hundred licensed taverns in Halifax and most of those on Barracks, George, and Albemarle Streets—with the full knowledge of authorities—were houses of ill repute. Fights, fires, and assaults were frequent and, though there was a brief period of calm following the riot of 1863, things soon returned to what was considered "normal" for that part of town and remained so for several generations to come.

12

THE BLACKBURN AFFAIR

(1865)

Conspiracy at the Halifax Hotel.

In April 1865, after the assassination of President Abraham Lincoln, word spread around the world of a previous attempt upon his life, and Halifax's reputation came under serious attack.

It all began less than two years earlier at the Queen's Hotel in Toronto. There, in December 1863, Dr. Luke P. Blackburn, a respected Kentucky physician and known Confederate agent, recruited a southern sympathizer, Godfrey Hyams, to help him kill as many Northerners as possible. A down-on-his-luck Englishman with a family to support, Hyams was promised sixty thousand dollars when the task was complete, and was told to continue in his job as a shoemaker until Blackburn sent him further instructions.

In February, Blackburn made his way to Halifax and took rooms at the smart Halifax Hotel on Hollis Street. There, over a period of about two weeks, he held clandestine meetings with prominent local men sympathetic to the Southern cause, including that notorious Southern agent Alexander Keith Jr.

Blackburn then moved on to Bermuda, where a yellow fever epidemic was raging. An expert in infectious diseases, he offered his assistance free of charge. In the months that followed, however, several nurses observed him engaging in strange behaviour—carefully gathering pieces of the soiled clothing of sick and dying patients and packing the items into steamer trunks.

Godfrey Hyams, meanwhile, had finally received his instructions. On June 18 he was met at the Halifax Hotel by Keith, who, on Blackburn's orders, was to take care of Hyams's expenses. But when Keith noticed Northern agents lurking about the lobby, he moved Hyams to the Farmers Hotel on Argyle Street where Michael Doran, the manager, was a co-conspirator.

Blackburn returned to Halifax on July 12 aboard the steamer *Alphia* and, despite Keith's concerns, chose to stay at the Halifax Hotel as the Farmers was simply not up to his standards. He sent for Hyams right away and introduced him to the second officer of the *Alphia*, a Mr. Hill, who had smuggled Blackburn's mysterious trunks to Halifax. Later that afternoon Hyams joined Hill at Cunard's Wharf where they loaded eight trunks and a leather valise into the back of a hired wagon. Five of the trunks had been tied with rope; these contained the infected clothing. Hyams took them back to the Farmers to be stored in Doran's private parlour. He delivered the other three and the valise to Blackburn at the Halifax, as they contained his personal property.

That's when Dr. Blackburn filled him in on the finer details of the plot.

The infected trunks, he said, were destined for Northern cities close to Union Army bases. Hyams was to take them to Boston, then ship them by express wagon to auction rooms in each designated city. Blackburn was confident that prospective buyers would insist upon opening them to inspect their contents, thus initiating the spread of infection. The trunks were so contagious, he said, that if he were forced to open them Hyams should protect himself by chewing camphor and smoking strong cigars.

The largest trunk—which Blackburn affectionately referred to as "Big Number Two"—was intended for Washington itself. Its contents, he said, were so deadly that everyone within sixty yards when it was opened would be killed.

The most important part of the plan, however, involved the leather valise.

This, he said, was a gift for President Lincoln and Hyams was to personally ensure that it was delivered to the White House. It contained several fine linen shirts, of a size that would fit Mr. Lincoln, and a letter, written supposedly by an acquaintance. Packed neatly beneath the shirts, however, was a blanket from the deathbed of a yellow fever victim that had been saturated with infectious fluids. This gift, Blackburn said, would ultimately kill the president and all other occupants of the White House.

Captain John O'Brien of the barque *Halifax* was pleased to accept a twenty-dollar gold piece for smuggling what he thought were five trunks of gifts for Hyams's family and friends and, with Hyams aboard, sailed for Boston on July 18. Soon after arriving, Hyams shipped the containers as instructed and returned to Toronto. After a second attempt to smuggle infected materials from Bermuda to Halifax failed, Blackburn also returned to Toronto. He and several colleagues continued to devise other schemes against the North and repeatedly ignored Hyams' demands for payment.

On April 9, 1865, the surrender of Robert E. Lee signalled the beginning of the end of the war. Within a week, the world was horrified by news of the assassination of Abraham Lincoln. That's when an angry Godfrey Hyams, with a guarantee of immunity, stepped forward to tell his story. Blackburn was arrested and tried for violating Canada's neutrality laws.

Daily reports of the trial in newspapers around the world portrayed Halifax as a hotbed of would-be assassins and

ne'er-do-wells, and caused fears within the community of ret-
ribution both physical and financial. Blackburn's trial, however,
ended in an acquittal. He was being tried only for violating
Canadian laws, not attempted assassination. And, as the trunks
themselves had never physically been on Canadian soil, the court
determined that Canadian law did not apply. Confederation was
still a few years away, and Nova Scotia was still a colony. No effort
was made to refer the matter to a British court.

During the trial, a related scandal erupted in Halifax.

A. J. Ritchie, the editor of the *Sun* newspaper, sparked an
uproar when he accused members of the Dalhousie University
Medical Faculty of complicity in the Blackburn affair. Dr. Ed
Jennings and Dr. John Slayter, he said, had met Blackburn at the
Halifax Hotel in February 1864 to advise him on the safe transfer
of infected materials from Bermuda. And, Ritchie said, the premier himself, Dr. Charles Tupper, had told him so.

Tupper denied the charge, claiming that Ritchie had misinter-
preted him. He himself had a reputation for stretching the truth,
however, and few believed him. Slayter and Jennings threatened
to sue the *Sun,* while the Medical Society conducted an investigation into the matter. The eventual conclusion was that it was
best to allow the affair to rest, rather than to further tarnish the
reputation of Halifax's medical community. When the Blackburn
trial ended, this matter also came to a close.

As it turned out, the yellow fever plot launched from Halifax
did not have the desired effect—at least, not completely. Some of
Blackburn's trunks were intercepted before reaching their destina-
tions and there is no record of the valise ever having been delivered
to the White House. The trunk sent to New Bern, North Carolina,
however, was believed at the time to have caused an outbreak of
yellow fever that resulted in more than two thousand deaths.

Blackburn eventually returned to Kentucky where he was welcomed as a hero; in September 1879, he was elected governor. He

died in 1887 and his tombstone reads "The Good Samaritan."

In 1902 it was proven that yellow fever can be transmitted only by mosquitoes.

13

THE *ZERO* MUTINY

(1865)

A piracy trial brings people to the streets.

From the time he was just a young lad, Henry Dowcey had a longing for adventure that just couldn't be found in the small village of Weymouth, Nova Scotia; in those rare moments when he wasn't labouring on his father's small patch of land, or helping his mother care for his younger brothers and sisters, he would sit on the edge of the dock watching vessels sail down the Sissiboo River toward the Bay of Fundy and the great wide world beyond.

One day, a trip to Halifax turned into the opportunity of a lifetime.

After a night of drinking, the cook of a cargo ship tumbled into the harbour and drowned, leaving the captain scrambling to find a replacement as the ship was about to raise anchor and head for the West Indies. On a whim, Dowcey applied and was taken on. He stayed with the ship for a few years, then joined the crew of HMS *Ariadne* as a civilian cook.

A shy young man, Henry quietly went about his work and kept himself to himself, but in early 1865, while *Ariadne* was stationed

in Jamaica, he made a friend—a redheaded Scot by the name of
John C. Douglas. Douglas, thirty years old, was five feet six inches
tall and stout, with flaming red hair and a full, bushy beard.
Though he professed to be a religious man, Douglas was quite
prepared to lie, cheat, or threaten bodily harm to get his way.
Dowcey, on the other hand, was from all accounts a reasonable,
if naïve fellow. He was black, five feet seven and a half inches in
height, physically fit, and clean-shaven.

In mid-summer, the two friends left *Ariadne* and set off in
search of adventure aboard a packet bound for New York City,
where, shortly after arriving, they learned that the brig *Zero* out
of Nova Scotia was in need of crew for its return voyage. For
Henry Dowcey, it was an opportunity to visit his home; for John
Douglas, Nova Scotia was as good a place as any to go next. With
papers in hand they set out for the dock in search of Captain
Colin C. Benson.

A comparatively small man who walked with a pronounced
limp, the forty-year-old master of the *Zero* was known in seafaring communities along the North Atlantic coast as an honest
and fair-minded man as well as an excellent judge of character.
Benson immediately took Henry Dowcey on as ship's cook,
though he disliked John Douglas on sight and twice refused to
hire him. But experienced sailors with Douglas's papers were in
short supply and, as the days slipped by and no others showed
any interest in the job, Benson was left with little choice but to
take Douglas on as mate.

The rest of the *Zero*'s crew was made up of two Swiss seamen
and fifteen-year-old cabin boy Frank Stockwell. The *Zero* set sail
for Cape Breton, where it was contracted to pick up a cargo of
coal for delivery to Boston. Along the way, Douglas was repeatedly insolent and argumentative, and soon proved to be less
competent at his job than his credentials indicated. For the first
time in his career, Benson felt uneasy aboard his own vessel.

When the *Zero* finally docked at Cow Bay, Cape Breton, (Port Morien) the Swiss seamen secured passage on a fishing boat to Lunenburg and Benson was once again shorthanded. Considering how much time had been wasted in New York, he had to quickly find replacements for the Swiss and for Douglas as well, as he didn't trust the man and wanted to be rid of him.

Benson told Douglas he was finished, set out for Glace Bay, and returned hours later with three men—two German seamen, William Lambrecht and Charley Marlbeyr, and a new mate, Donald McIver. Unfortunately, soon after arriving at the *Zero*, McIver had a change of heart and left without notice. With time at a premium, Benson had no choice but to keep Douglas after all. On the evening of Thursday, September 7, 1865, the fully loaded *Zero* set sail.

Four days later, about a quarter mile off the mouth of the LaHave River, Nova Scotia, local fishermen encountered a drifting brig. After attaching a line and climbing on board they discovered evidence of a failed attempt to scuttle the vessel. The helm had been lashed tight and though the foresail, mainsail, jibs, and other sails remained intact, the sides had been cut through to the beams with an ax and several holes had been bored into the vessel below the waterline. The captain's cabin had been ransacked and his trunk turned out. After scraping away black paint hastily splashed over the ship's name, they learned they were on the *Zero*. It appeared that Captain Colin Benson and his crew had fallen prey to pirates, and word of the tragedy spread quickly through the seafaring community. The only sign of life on board was Benson's small dog.

The next morning, locals reported that members of the *Zero*'s crew had been seen in town, unaware that their ship had been found, and claiming that Captain Benson had fallen overboard and drowned. Within the hour, arrest warrants were issued.

On October 7, when the packet *Viper* docked at Wainwright's

Wharf in Halifax, dozens of angry people were waiting. For days, local newspapers had been reporting on an act of piracy aboard the brig *Zero* in the waters off LaHave and the murder of its popular captain, Colin Benson. On board the *Viper*, in the custody of Halifax police sergeant Lewis Hutt, were three of the five accused men. The others had already been picked up on the road to Windsor and were occupying a cell at the County Jail.

The crowd jeered and taunted the mutineers as they were loaded into a barred prison wagon, and followed it along city streets until it reached Spring Garden Road and turned into the yard of the County Jail, directly behind the courthouse.

On October 31 at 10:30 a.m., Henry Dowcey, John Douglas, and William Lambrecht were arraigned on charges of murder on the high seas. Charges against the others had already been dropped as they had agreed to turn over queen's evidence.

The trial began on November 10 and interest was so high that, well before dawn, dozens of townspeople began gathering near the front steps of the courthouse. When the doors finally opened at nine o'clock, a large crowd streamed into the building and up the stairs to fill every available seat in the courtroom. Presiding was the former premier, Chief Justice Sir William Young.

Sergeant Lewis Hutt presented physical evidence in the form of the captain's gold watch, which he had recovered in Liverpool from a man who said that Dowcey had exchanged it for a silver one plus five dollars in cash. Articles of clothing found in Dowcey's trunk were identified as being the property of Benson as well. The fishermen who found the abandoned vessel described for the court the state of the *Zero* and their belief that there had been an attempt to scuttle it. And both Frank Stockwell and Charley Marlbeyr told the court that Douglas had orchestrated the entire tragedy by manipulating Dowcey into beating the captain about the head with a belaying pin, and then forcing Lambrecht to help toss him overboard.

Closing arguments were held on Saturday morning, November 11, and at 4:45 p.m. the jury returned to present its verdict before a packed courtroom. Dowcey and Douglas were found guilty of murder on the high seas. Lambrecht was found not guilty and released.

Ever since the story of the *Zero* mutiny first appeared in Halifax newspapers in mid-September, the public had been caught up in the drama. The German and black communities, in particular, were concerned that, as minorities in what was largely a white British environment, Dowcey and Lambrecht were at a distinct disadvantage. Both communities actively raised funds to pay for the defence. Large contingents from each were present through-out the trial and actively lobbied politicians, clergy, or anyone else who would listen.

On Thursday, November 30, Haligonians again descended on the courthouse in large numbers to witness the sentencing. The courtroom, corridors, and stairways were filled to capacity while many people milled about outside on Spring Garden Road. One spectator, after making it all the way into a coveted seat, fainted and had to be passed out over the heads of the crowd.

Handcuffed together, Dowcey and Douglas were led into the courtroom and placed in the prisoners' dock. Justice Young announced that on this day only Dowcey would be sentenced, as the court was required to consider a last-minute argument by the counsel for Douglas. Dowcey was asked if he had anything to say before sentence was pronounced, and, as he did not, the chief justice (reportedly with tears in his eyes) said to him:

> ...*The sentence of the Court is that you be taken back to the place from whence you came, and thence be carried to such place within this County, and... that you be there hanged by the neck until you are dead, and may God have mercy on your soul.*"

The words evoked no visible emotion in Dowcey and, as the doors opened and spectators began to inch their way out of the room, he and Douglas were returned to their cells. Outside, on Spring Garden Road, clusters of men gathered to complain about the deferral of the mate's sentence. Most felt that he was as guilty as the cook and that the jury's verdict should have been put into full effect immediately.

Over the Christmas holidays, five judges—Chief Justice Young and Judges Dodd, desBarres, Johnston and Wilkins—considered the argument of Douglas' defence counsel, which was that since he did not commit the murder with his own hands he was not as guilty as Dowcey, and should not suffer the same punishment. The judges returned to the court with their decision on January 3, 1866.

Chief Justice Young and Judges Dodd and desBarres all agreed with the verdict of the jury, while Judges Johnston and Wilkins did not. The majority carried, however, and the prisoner was asked if he had anything to say before sentence was pronounced. Douglas went into a lengthy and at times erratic denial of his own guilt, professing a deep religious conviction that would not have allowed him to harm another living creature and claiming that both Germans had been involved with the cook in the plot to kill the captain. He had not said so earlier for fear that Dowcey would carry out a threat to kill him. In a further appeal for mercy, he claimed to be the only son and therefore the only support of his widowed mother, who was in ill health and living in Scotland.

As Douglas stood shaking in the dock, the chief justice (this time with apparently not a shred of remorse) sentenced him to death. A quick appeal to the governor, however, resulted in the sentence being commuted to life at hard labour at the Northwest Arm Penitentiary.

A storm of public protest followed. It was clear, people said, that Douglas was the prime instigator of this sad affair and that, though there was no doubt of his guilt, Dowcey deserved as much consideration. Politicians, clergy, and prominent and ordinary citizens alike became involved in the argument. Archbishop Connolly, for example, sent letters to members of the legislature and to the editors of newspapers protesting that, while he was not personally opposed to the death penalty, in this case there was no justification for hanging one of the criminals and not the other.

People took to the streets, surrounded Province House, and demanded equal justice. Death or life at hard labour, each man deserved the same fate.

A petition to the same effect, with six thousand signatures, was presented to the Executive Council, and, though they accepted it graciously, they deferred to the Governor whose decision was allowed to stand. Protests at Government House followed, but to no avail.

Every newspaper in Halifax reflected the outrage over the sentence imposed on Dowcey. The *Morning Chronicle*, on January 20, 1866, for example, reported, *"Never was condemnation of a single act more unanimous. All shades of religion, of politics, and of color unite in general indignation."*

THE EXECUTION

For many years, a dark green fence of tall wooden planks enclosed the yard behind the courthouse, securing the County Jail. At the Spring Garden Road entrance, a gate—also made of wooden planks—contained a locked door, above which a neat hand-lettered sign read, "GAOL."

Shortly before daybreak on the morning of January 24 the gate was unlocked and, as an armed guard stood nearby, invited observers began to arrive and were shown to a reserved area in the yard. Among the first were the city marshal and his deputy in the company of thirty constables. Four companies of the 17th Regiment soon followed, marching into the yard behind an officer on horseback to take positions near the scaffold—two at the west side and two at the east— to prevent the crowd from pressing too close.

The scaffold was constructed of rough lumber and stood next to the fence at the rear of the yard on the east side of the jail building. Its supporting beams were eighteen feet high; the platform, measuring about nine feet by four feet was about eight feet off the ground; and the trap was fourteen inches higher than the platform. A series of crudely constructed steps led to the top and on the ground beneath the platform was a wooden coffin, painted black. About 6 a.m. the hangman—a short, thickset man calling himself "Smith" and wearing a black scarf over a face that had already been smeared with bootblack—walked into the yard and quickly slipped under the platform amid murmurs of contempt from those who saw him. It was believed that he was a stranger to the city, a sailor who had agreed to take on an ugly job, for a price.

At 6:30 a.m., the mayor and a number of aldermen were escorted to their assigned places, and representatives of local newspapers were positioned where they could clearly observe the proceedings. Members of the public also began to arrive, though due to the early hour the numbers were not as great as expected. The *Morning Chronicle* reported later that there were *"probably not more than one hundred and fifty present, exclusive of the military and constables."* The branches of trees just beyond the fence, however, were weighed down with dozens of spectators anxious to get a first-hand look.

Dowcey had been awake for most of the night in the company of two Catholic priests. When the time came he stood and, with his arms bound tightly behind him, stepped outside into the cold morning air. It was three minutes past seven o'clock. Seeing him, the officer on horseback cried, *"Attention!"* and *"Fix bayonets!"* drawing the eyes of the spectators to the doorway. A hush descended over the yard as the condemned man and his priests made their way to the scaffold steps.

After reading the judgment against him, the high sheriff offered Dowcey the chance to speak before the drop fell, and the yard became very still as observers strained to hear the condemned man deliver his final words:

> *Gentlemen, I tell you that I was not the instigator of Captain Benson's death. I am sorry for what I have done. I regret that I deprived poor Captain Benson of his life, but I tell you that I was hard pushed to do it by a man you all know. He urged me to do it and pushed me very hard. If it had not been for this person, I would not be in the position I am in today. I repeat that I am very sorry for what I have done, but had it not been for that man I would not be compelled to give up my blood today. But Gentlemen, I say, God for us all.*

When he had finished, Dowcey stepped beneath the noose, stared straight ahead, and stood very still as a white cap that was just long enough to cover his eyes was pulled over his head. The hangman, sheriff and priests then descended the platform, leaving him to his fate. The hangman took his place beneath the scaffold, his hand poised over the bolt of the trap, waiting for the sheriff's signal to pull. A minute later, the bolt was drawn and Henry Dowcey shot through the trap door, his body twisting and convulsing for some minutes. The noose had been incorrectly tied, leaving him to slowly strangle. The crowd was horrified and so angry at the sight that the hangman made a hasty exit and was last seen running down Bishop Street toward the docks.

At twenty-four minutes past seven, death was pronounced.

In June, the remains of Donald McIver—the man that Captain Benson had hired months earlier to replace John Douglas as mate—were discovered in the water near the Gowrie Mines wharf at Cow Bay, Cape Breton. He had last been seen boarding the ill-fated *Zero* in the company of two of the crew.

As for John Douglas, he remained at the Northwest Arm Penitentiary until he died of a fever at the age of forty-two. When his body was turned over to the Dalhousie Medical School to be used for anatomical specimens, those who knew him claimed that it was the first useful thing to have come from his miserable life.

14

THE LIBRARIAN

(1879)

Outrage at the city market.

A farmers' market has operated in Halifax since its earliest days, and for close to two centuries it was located off Hollis Street in an area known as Cheapside (named for one of the principal markets of London, England).

One day a week, farmers would come to town with wagon loads of produce, meat, and handmade wares such as brooms, tools, and furnishings, while fishermen would carry their goods up from the docks. Stalls lined both sides of George Street from the Grand Parade to Water Street, and ran along Hollis Street as far as Prince Street, then around the corner and along the length of Bedford Row. For generations of Haligonians, this was the place to do the weekly grocery shopping.

In 1879, John Thomas Bulmer could look out upon the marketplace from his office in the Legislative Library of Province House. He was the first provincial librarian and, like his friends and neighbours, he was a regular customer of the market.

Bulmer had been born in 1856 on a small farm in Nappan

Station, Nova Scotia. Bright, with a keen interest in learning, young John was constantly astounding his family with his grand ideas and his determination to see them fulfilled. After graduating from the Amherst Academy in 1871, he set out for Halifax with the intention of becoming a lawyer, and, after articling for four years, was called to the bar on July 21, 1875.

When he wasn't engaged in academic pursuits, Bulmer's days were filled with the practice of criminal law and countless efforts at social reform, and, as he was an avid bibliophile, an almost obsessive need to improve the standards of local libraries. It was his love of books and education that prompted him to visit some of the most prominent academic institutions in North America, and from the librarians of Yale, Harvard, and Columbia he learned the essentials of stocking and running a modern library.

Remarkably, in July 1877, amid his cases, projects, and causes, he found the time to get married and to set up a home in Halifax with his bride, Eleanor Jane McHeffey, at 3 Brier Lane, a small street that ran off South Park Street, opposite the Public Gardens.

Bulmer raised his three sons to appreciate education, professional integrity, and the need for social reform. He was a man of strong opinions, with a caustic wit and such eloquence that his listeners were often left clamouring for more. If he believed a cause was worth fighting for, regardless of its popularity or lack thereof, he embraced it wholeheartedly. To his opponents he was stubborn and arrogant, but to those who knew him best—his friends and family—he was an incurable idealist.

During his early years in Halifax, Bulmer became acquainted with several other bright young lawyers, among them Robert Sedgewick and Benjamin Russell, and together they formed a discussion group called "The Halifax Law Society." The primary concern of this collection of young friends was the lack of consistent professional standards in far too many of the lawyers then in practice. To them, this was a clear indication of the need for a law school at Dalhousie University, and, though several early attempts failed, they never gave up hope. In 1883, critical support came in the form of an endowment from publisher and philanthropist George Munro, and the Dalhousie Law School came into being.

For John Bulmer, this was just one undertaking of many. In 1879, after having been instrumental in establishing the Nova Scotia Historical Society, he was given the opportunity to put his library skills to the test as the first salaried provincial librarian. His immediate challenge was the Legislative Library, which had been allowed to deteriorate alarmingly. In just three years under his direction, it grew from six thousand volumes in various stages of disrepair to twenty-five thousand volumes that included rare and historic periodicals along with many valuable first editions. The Legislative Library had become one of the best and largest libraries in the country.

Bulmer was particularly proud of the collection of historic newspapers that he had compiled, from the first edition, in 1752, of the *Halifax Gazette,* and including every edition of this and every other Halifax newspaper that followed. He saw this as an invaluable social record that would undoubtedly be an important resource to current and future historians.

He accomplished all of this at no public expense, demonstrating great skill at bartering, exchanging, and attracting donations. It was as a result of this success that, in 1882, the Nova Scotia government agreed to his request for a paid assistant. Over his strenuous objections, however, they gave the post to an untrained person with political connections. Disgusted, Bulmer abruptly tendered his resignation and returned full time to the practice of law.

His anger over the circumstances of his departure surfaced a few months later. In January 1883, at the city market across the street from Province House, Bulmer happened upon fishmongers and butchers wrapping their goods in the pages of historic newspapers and periodicals—publications that he personally had acquired for the Legislative Library! Furious, he gathered up every one of the publications that he could find and, within hours, his outrage over actions apparently taken by his successor, Francis Blake Crofton, was causing a stir.

In the days that followed, Haligonians were stopping members of the legislature on the street to complain about their choice of successor to Bulmer, and that pressure, combined with the efforts of the Nova Scotia Historical Society, convinced the library commissioners to conduct an investigation.

For a time it appeared as though Crofton might lose his job, but his name was ultimately cleared when the blame was placed on a house messenger named Coleman, who Crofton claimed had been ordered to sell only "duplicate" periodicals to victuallers and the like. Crofton claimed that, in an effort to make extra money for himself, Coleman had sold the remaining publications as well. His explanation did not satisfy Bulmer, however, who saw no justification for selling off the very few duplicates in question and firmly believed that Coleman was simply being made a scapegoat for Crofton's bad decision.

Months later, as the members of the Halifax Law Society eagerly awaited the opening of the Dalhousie Law School, Bulmer was urged to accept the post of school librarian. With his legal training and a proven expertise in library management, he was perfectly suited for the job. He agreed without hesitation. The opportunity to combine his love of education, books, and the law was simply too good to pass up.

As with everything else in his life, he set about creating the new library with great enthusiasm and was soon on his way to acquiring a substantial collection. In no time at all he had created a library that was far superior to that of any other faculty at the university; though after only a year in the position he was informed, with great regret, that the school could no longer afford to pay his salary. That, however, did not stop him. He took this as an opportunity to further his own legal education and enrolled in classes from 1884 to 1885, during which time he continued to act, as time permitted, as a voluntary librarian.

For the rest of his days he maintained a proprietary interest in the law school library, trusting that, at the very least, he had laid a solid foundation for future librarians to build upon. Such was his affection for the school itself that in 1896, during an effort to bring about a Canadian Bar Association, he declared that in his considered opinion the Dalhousie Law School offered the best legal education in the entire country.

One of John Bulmer's most impressive aspects was his instinctive need to bring about social reform. From the early days of his career he was a steadfast champion of the black community in its fight for equality. In 1876, when the City of Halifax implemented a policy of segregation in public schools, for example, he and Robert Sedgewick, who was at the time a member of the Board of School Commissioners, became actively involved in the fight to have the policy rescinded. In 1884, after a bitter struggle, they succeeded. In the 1890s he saw great promise in a young law student—James Robinson Johnston, the Dalhousie school's first black graduate—and, in 1900, took him into his own practice to complete his studies.

Bulmer's sense of justice was offended not only by racism, but also by the mistreatment of the poor, by the inequality of women, and by the detrimental effects of the consumption of alcohol. When, in 1887, he decided to run as a prohibition candidate in the federal election, it came as no surprise to those who knew him. Though he lost to prominent Conservative candidate Charles Tupper, he wasn't discouraged. He simply took a different approach and founded a weekly magazine, *Canadian Voice (Halifax)*, through which he advocated support for the causes he cared so passionately about, including women's suffrage and equal pay for men and women for jobs of equal value. In these respects, he was a man well ahead of his time.

John Thomas Bulmer passed away suddenly at the age of fifty-five on February 9, 1901, leaving Eleanor, their three sons, and many friends to mourn his loss. In his lifetime, he had struggled to make a difference. He wasn't always successful, and the successes he had certainly didn't make him a wealthy man, but in his own way he accomplished much; and his cherished library was his valuable legacy to several generations of law students.

Friend or foe, no one could deny that John Thomas Bulmer made an impact.

15

ESPRIT DE CORPS

(1880)

A soldier's scheme goes awry.

Through the wars of three centuries, Halifax's economy was largely dependent upon the military. It boomed during wartime, with the arrival and departure of the king's ships and thousands of men, and suffered during the periods of peace that followed.

Any benefits to a garrison town, however, were often outweighed by its troubles.

Property damage or personal assaults against civilians by drunken soldiers or sailors counted among the most frequent of crimes, and there seemed little will on the part of military authorities to punish those responsible. Military crimes were different. Any soldier who dared to defy an order, or appeared drunk on duty, or committed an assault against another soldier could face swift and brutal justice. Captured deserters, for example, soon found themselves dancing for the king at the end of a rope.

Though the sensibilities of the civilian population usually carried little weight, in the summer of 1880 the behaviour of some "recent drafts" of the famous and well-respected 97th Regiment so angered the people of Halifax that the authorities were actually forced to take action.

In August 1880, two soldiers—Samuel White and Richard Foster—were confined to barracks at the Citadel, charged with misconduct. It wasn't a new experience for either. Foster had recently been tried for the burglary of a civilian's house and, though he had been (of course) acquitted, the incident had served only to further tarnish an already questionable reputation. White was no better and had been disciplined more times than he could remember.

Both men had tired of the restrictive nature of military service, and there were only three ways out: desertion, court martial, or being killed in battle. Court martial was an obvious preference and so these two ne'er-do-wells came up with a plan they believed would lead to their swift discharge from the regiment.

On Friday August 27 at 9:50 p.m., with the corporal of the guard, Flinter, busy at the gate, the two men slipped unseen away from the fort. They headed straight down George Street to the Parade Square and on to Hollis Street where, at the corner of Prince Street they took off their belts, and, twisting them with the buckles out, began deliberately breaking plate glass windows of the shops along the east side of Hollis, and didn't stop until they reached Sackville Street. In less than ten minutes, about five hundred square feet of glass, valued at fifteen hundred dollars, was broken.

One shocked bystander ran off in search of the police. A doctor who had been watching from a window of the Halifax Club across the street ran out to try and stop the destruction. For his trouble he was assaulted by one of the soldiers and, while a few passers-by came to his aid, not one was willing to take the same risk. Minutes later, Constable John Nickerson arrived and arrested the soldiers without resistance. It seemed that White and Foster's plan was working! Witnesses reported later that while both men acted drunk, it appeared to be a ruse, for neither gave a believable performance.

As the *Morning Herald* put it in on October 11, 1880,

> *Discussing the dastardly conduct of the scoundrels of the 97th in smashing valuable glass in Hollis Street windows, a well known citizen suggests that "the whole regiment should be reigned up and shot as an example."*

The magistrate, weary of hearing complaints about the behaviour of military men, committed them to stand trial before Chief Justice Sir William Young of the Supreme Court. Their wish to be released from the regiment was soon realized—with a sentence of eight years at hard labour at the Northwest Arm Penitentiary. The penitentiary closed soon after and the men were shipped off to a new facility at Dorchester, New Brunswick to finish their term.

For his part, the corporal of the Guard, Flinter, was placed under arrest and tried by court martial for neglect of duty. He was sentenced to several months of hard labour at the Melville Island Military Prison.

The good reputation of the 97th would soon receive another blow. On October 9, soldier Henry Mayhew was not drunk and did not pretend to be when he entered the porch of the Waverley House Inn on Pleasant Street (now Barrington) and with a walking cane began to deliberately break windows. Three valuable stained-glass panes were destroyed before the police arrived to arrest Mayhew and take him away. He was examined at the police court on October 11 and subsequently turned over to military authorities, and unfortunately for Mayhew, the military authorities were feeling pressure from within to restore the regiment's honour.

On October 15, Mayhew was fined one dollar and had his pay docked at a rate of a penny a day until the damages were covered—taking him about eight years to clear the debt. But the most difficult part of his sentence—ninety-six weeks at hard labour—was served at the military prison on Melville Island, a severe punishment that would take every ounce of a man's strength to get through.

After arriving at the island and handing his papers over to the chief warder in charge, Mayhew was taken to the wash house to have his head shaved—a standard requirement for any prisoner serving eight weeks or more. Then, for the next twenty-three months, he followed a gruelling routine.

Each morning, Mayhew rose at dawn and, after ablutions and breakfast, faced his first task of the day. "Shot exercise" consisted of taking a twelve-pound shot from a stool, carrying it thirty-five yards, then taking it back—all the while keeping a steady pace. This carried on without pause for the next four hours, under the watchful eye of an armed guard. After a short rest, Mayhew began his next task, "heavy pack drill." For two hours he was made to march back and forth in a measured space with an extremely heavy pack on his back—under the orders of a non-commissioned officer who could, at will, order an "ordinary step," a "quick march," or a "double quick."

At the end of these six hours of punishment, Mayhew was only halfway through his workday. Over the next six hours he "picked oakum"—unravelling old ropes and preparing the fibres for use as caulking between the timbers of ships. By the time he sat down for his evening meal his fingers would be bleeding, and he would be almost too exhausted to eat. Mayhew followed this gruelling routine six days a week every week for almost two years. His only break from the monotony was the Sabbath.

As if the events of the preceding months hadn't been bad enough, the famed 97th was made to suffer another humiliation in the midst of the Mayhew trial. A plot by several lawless members of the regiment—to attack Halifax and destroy everything in their path—had been discovered. The major general commanding had to take immediate steps to protect the citizens, who were understandably nervous at the thought of bands of armed young men roaming the streets and attacking their property or their persons.

Security patrols were increased, and only men of good conduct were allowed to leave their barracks unless they were on duty. The uprising was averted. As the *Morning Herald* reported on October 12, *"We are assured that the officers and men of the regiment view with abhorrence the conduct of those who have brought disgrace on the regiment and will do all in their power to prevent any repetition."*

The reputation of the 97th Regiment was seriously damaged by these incidents and, in 1880, as it was preparing to depart Halifax for the last time, feelings in the city were mixed. While conceding that the majority of the regiment were honourable and orderly men and among the best in the British Army, most of the townspeople lamented the destruction caused by new recruits who did not possess the same *esprit de corps* as the veterans. The residents were not sad to see those new men go.

16

THE DYNAMITERS

(1883)

The heir to the throne escapes with his life.

Through the wars of the eighteenth and nineteenth centuries, Halifax was one of the most heavily armed military bases on the North Atlantic and in that time not one shot was fired on it in anger. In 1883, however, an event occurred that not only threatened the security of this military town, but the very heart of the British Empire—its royal family.

In May 1883, a sudden increase in military activity was the primary topic of conversation in the city's pubs, shops, and drawing rooms. Some spoke of seeing warships towing barges laden with guns, shells, and lumber to each of the forts overlooking the harbour where, as others noted, palisades had been erected almost overnight. City police were placed on full alert and a further seven police officers were sworn in by City Marshall Garret Cotter to stand guard at night over Province House, Government House, and the post office.

There was also talk of a mysterious letter, supposedly written to Lieutenant Governor Archibald by Sir John A. Macdonald, warning that a Fenian attack was imminent. Formed in the mid-nineteenth century, the Fenians were revolutionists, determined to free Ireland from British rule by using any means at their disposal. From the relative safety of the United States they had been able to carry out several violent raids into the nearest British territory, Canada.

Though military and naval authorities were not as forthcoming, the lieutenant governor freely admitted that a warning letter had been received from "a most reliable authority." The message advised that two armed vessels manned by Fenians and carrying a quantity of explosives had sailed from Boston a few days earlier, with the intention of mining Halifax Harbour. General Sir Patrick McDougal, commander in chief of British troops in North America stated that, in his view, the mining of the city as well as the harbour would not be difficult for the anarchists to carry out. He noted particularly that, if they chose, they could quite easily enter the storm drain at Freshwater River Bridge (near what is now the corner of Barrington and Inglis Streets) and, through the drain, lay a string of electrically charged mines into the heart of the city.

The Fenian ships did not appear, but a second letter in late September to the new lieutenant governor, Matthew Richey, put the army, navy, and police on full alert once again. It warned of the departure from New York City for Halifax of a person or persons who were in league with the Fenians, or the Dynamite Party.

On October 12, two men took a room at the Parker House Hotel on Barrington Street and almost immediately the proprietor, John Creelman, began to have doubts about them. Neither man had a job and yet they spent money freely, and though they claimed to be strangers to the city, a number of visitors had arrived at the hotel looking for them. Creelman expressed his concerns to Detective Nicholas Power, who had a reputation as the most respected and successful detective in the entire province.

Considering the current heightened state of security in Halifax, Power decided to look into the men's activities.

The next day, in the company of a policeman named Condon, Power went to Parker House to speak to James Holmes and William Bracken. They weren't in, but Power asked Creelman to open the room. The lock of one of two valises found near the bed was broken, and when Condon placed it on the bed, it readily opened. Power looked inside.

Beneath a blue shirt was a canvas parcel containing packages of a gray material that Power suspected was dynamite; but, as he didn't have a warrant, he returned the cases to where he had found them and went to City Marshal Cotter with his concerns. Cotter returned to the room with him and under his authority, one of the packages was removed and taken to Reynold's Hardware store. The clerk there confirmed that it was indeed dynamite, but not just any dynamite. It was known as "triple charge" dynamite, an expensive and highly effective form of the explosive that was most often used for marine purposes.

Detective Power arrested Holmes on Barrington Street just outside the hotel and charged him with being in possession of explosives contrary to law. Holmes denied any knowledge of the dynamite or of William Bracken. While Constable Condon escorted Holmes to the police station, Power—acting on a tip from an interested bystander—set off for John Cahill's bar on Lower Water Street where, he was told, he could find Bracken arguing with a bunch of locals about the state of Irish and American politics.

The arrival of Power in the midst of that conversation caught Bracken by surprise, and while he was being placed under arrest, he, too, denied having a roommate or possessing any dynamite. John Cahill gave Power a revolver that Bracken had left behind the bar.

At the police station, Cotter and Power began their interrogation. Despite distinct Irish accents, Holmes, the taller of the two, said he was born in Missouri and Bracken claimed to be a native of New York State. Both appeared to be about thirty years of age. Realizing that there was no longer any point in denying their possession of dynamite, the men said they were miners and that the explosives, which they had purchased in New York City, were simply tools of their trade.

Both, however, were at a loss to explain some of their other possessions. In Holmes's pockets, for example, Cotter found a copy of *Irish World* (a New York newspaper sympathetic to Fenians), nine dynamite cartridges (blasting caps), a supply of bullets, and two loaded guns: a five-chambered revolver and a four-chambered gun. The guns' barrels had been removed and placed in a strongly made square attachment. Both Cotter and Power knew that this device could be used to explode dynamite. In Bracken's pockets they found ten dynamite cartridges and keys to the valises that had been found in the hotel room.

Along with the men's overcoats, the valises were brought to Marshal Cotter's office for examination. In addition to some personal items, the valises held about eighty pounds of dynamite, several lengths of fuse, a keyhole saw, a hammer, grease, a coil of copper wire, a large gimlet, a grapnel hook, and two small round clocks, the alarms of which had been removed and replaced by devices that could pull a wire at the hour set. The explosives and equipment were then transported under guard to Hosterman's Magazine on the Northwest Arm for safekeeping.

The contents of Holmes's overcoat gave the strongest indication of who these men really were. In its pockets, Cotter found what appeared to be a Fenian reference manual, a newspaper article on how Fenian admirals were preparing to attack Victoria, BC, and notes on a Fenian fundraiser. There was also a baggage check for the North End station of the Windsor & Annapolis Railway. Cotter sent a policeman to collect whatever had been checked.

Meanwhile, Detective Power learned that Holmes and Bracken had actually arrived in Halifax several months earlier. The operator of one of many taverns on Lower Water Street, Charles Robinson, told him that they had taken one of his rooms in early July, after arriving at Halifax aboard a steamer from Boston. They had with them two valises and a large round parcel wrapped in canvas. Of particular interest to Power was the news that Holmes and Bracken had rented a boat for two days, and on both occasions had stayed out on the harbour until well after dark. A few days later, Robinson told them, the canvas-wrapped parcel had been picked up by a wagon from the Intercolonial Express. On an evening in mid-August, he said, they gave up their room and told him they were hiking to Richmond, so that they could catch the early morning train out of Halifax.

As it turned out, they went no further than 71 Dresden Row and the home of a coachman, Dennis Mehan, whose wife took in boarders. As she had no vacant rooms, they agreed to share with one other person, John O'Donnell, who later told Power that the men had had a visitor during the few weeks they stayed at the Mehan house—a fellow named Joe, who was an engineer and appeared to be an American.

Joe stayed a few days, he said, sleeping on the floor between the beds, and on at least one occasion had accompanied Holmes and Bracken to their jobs at the Freshwater River Bridge (which was the location of that storm drain that General MacDougal had earlier expressed concern about). Mrs. Mehan told Power that they quit that job soon after and had gone to work at the Richmond railway yard. Before heading for Richmond, Power ordered an inspection of the drain. After ensuring it had not yet been mined, he alerted the military authorities. Men from the Halifax Volunteer Brigade formed an around-the-clock guard.

At the rail yard, foremen John Burns and William Brewitt told Power that the two men had been hired on September 6 to dig a trench; and, though they claimed to be experienced gold miners, the work was obviously far too strenuous for them. On September 13, they resigned. Soon after, they left Mrs. Mehan's establishment and their whereabouts between then and October 12, when they turned up at the Parker House, could not be ascertained, although it was believed they had gone to New Brunswick.

In the meantime, the baggage claim found in Holmes's possession revealed the canvas-wrapped package sent from Mr. Robinson's tavern in July. Inside was a modern rubber inflatable diving suit that appeared to have been used at least once.

Vice Admiral Edmund Commerell was among those who were informed of the arrest and investigation, and in the company of Lieutenant Paul Bush, the torpedo lieutenant of HMS *Northampton,* he went to Hosterman's Magazine to review the evidence. Both concluded that the explosives and equipment were ideally suited for an assault against shipping. Upon learning from Detective Power that the prisoners had spent a week working near the beach at Richmond, that they had spent two days on the harbour, and that they had possession of a diving suit, Commerell felt their intent was clear.

Extra guard boats were ordered for the protection of six Royal Navy warships moored in the harbour. Their destruction would have suited the Fenians very well, but Commerell believed there was an even more sinister purpose to their plan. Serving as a midshipman aboard one of the ships, HMS *Canada,* was none other than eighteen-year-old Prince George (later King George V) and the assassination of a member of the royal family would have struck a blow against Britain like no other.

Within days young Prince George was sent off to the West Indies, out of harm's way, and Canadian government officials joined military and naval authorities in offering their congratulations to Cotter and Power.

Over the course of the trial, which began in November,

courtroom seating was at a premium. Military and naval officials, along with several politicians, left little room for the general public. Bail was set at six thousand dollars each plus sureties of three thousand dollars each, effectively guaranteeing that Holmes and Bracken would stay in jail. While the defence presented them as miners with a legitimate reason for carrying dynamite, experts like John Smith of Reynold's Hardware and Benjamin Wilson of the Acadia Powder Works testified that the dynamite in question was designed for marine work and they knew of no underwater mining in Nova Scotia. An additional charge of smuggling was brought, as there were no customs records to support the prisoners' claim that they had purchased the dynamite in the United States.

Every newspaper in the region had reporters in the gallery and their reports covered the trial in great detail.

Holmes and Bracken appeared nervous as they waited for Justice Thompson of the Supreme Court to pronounce sentence. Instead of the lengthy term they might have expected, however, they were fortunate to be returned to prison for just another six months. As the judge pointed out, they were charged only with the possession of dynamite and smuggling, and not with the more serious crimes they may have intended to commit. Thompson felt he was left with little other choice.

After their release on October 30, Holmes and Bracken returned to the United States—but not before making the astonishing admission to a few locals that if they had not been stopped, the young prince's blood would have most assuredly been on their hands and the people of Halifax would have had good reason to remember the Fenian cause.

On March 30, 1915, in the Legislative Chamber of Province House, Lieutenant Governor James Drummond McGregor presided over a ceremony honouring retired Police Chief Nicholas Power, during which he was presented with the King's Police

Medal for a lifetime of meritorious service and for effectively preventing the assassination of a future king.

Honourable M. H. Goudge led the gathering in three rousing cheers for the king and three more for Nicholas Power.

17

THE IMPRISONMENT OF MAYOR THOMAS

(1892)

A partisan challenges the premier and loses...
temporarily.

In May 1890, the election of Frederick A. Laurence, the town recorder of Truro, Nova Scotia, as a Liberal member of the legislature was an unpleasant surprise to the very conservative Mayor David J. Thomas and his council. But, they had to concede, having one of their own town officials sitting on the government side of the House of Assembly might be a good thing—if they could only tolerate his political affiliation.

In the late nineteenth century, members of the legislature made very little in way of salary and most had to keep their regular jobs. Mr. Laurence, a lawyer, continued as town recorder (town clerk/magistrate) long after he had been elected.

Two years later, Mayor Thomas and his council saw Mr. Laurence in an even more negative light when a letter arrived from Premier William Stevens Fielding's office ordering them to substantially increase the salary of the town recorder. In an answering letter, the mayor assured the premier that the town was not in a position to increase the recorder's salary, and had no intention of doing so. By way of return letter, the premier impressed upon him that he had absolutely no choice in the matter.

Now, it had been common practice for successive governments—both Liberal and Conservative—to exert similar pressures on the employers of members of the legislature wherever they could. This was one of the few ways to properly compensate MLAs for travelling back and forth to Halifax and for carrying out their constituency business. The premier and his cabinet knew that if they gave in to Mayor Thomas they risked setting a precedent.

Mayor Thomas was furious, and with every perceived affront his vehement dislike of Liberals increased. All over town, he complained about the audacity of the government to make such an outrageous demand on the people of Truro! As a successful merchant, he said, he knew the value of a dollar, and Mr. Laurence deserved no more than he was already getting—especially considering how much time he spent in Halifax as a part of that Liberal government! Thomas and his council decided to take matters into their own hands.

Word soon reached the Legislature that they had drawn up a petition accusing Mr. Laurence of using his position to get an increase in salary, then reached out to every man in town eligible to vote. Mr. Laurence was not amused. He felt that his reputation was being unfairly tarnished and, as repeated attempts at reasoning with the mayor came to nothing, he took the matter directly to the premier and his cabinet colleagues.

As a result, the Thomas-Laurence conflict came before the House of Assembly in the form of a government resolution, and since the Liberals had a majority, the outcome was never in doubt.

The members concluded by majority vote that Mr. Thomas had committed a libellous act and had breached the privilege of the House. The very next day, the sergeant-at-arms delivered a summons to Thomas, requiring him to present himself to the House to explain his actions.

Mayor Thomas—Welsh by birth and stubborn by nature—knew he had to comply and set off for Halifax in a determined mood. If the premier and his cabinet tried to browbeat him into backing down (and he fully expected they would) they were in for a rude awakening. David James Thomas could not be easily intimidated.

He arrived in Halifax late in the day, and after spending the night at the home of a friend, arrived fresh and ready to do battle at Province House the next morning. The sergeant-at-arms escorted him to the Legislative Chamber door, announced his arrival, and led him into the room. Over the next hour, Thomas stated his case—though barely able to contain his frustration—and politely but firmly answered all of the questions that were fired at him. Finally, the premier adjourned the meeting and asked Mayor Thomas to step outside while he and his cabinet deliberated amongst themselves. The sergeant-at-arms, they said, would call him when they were ready to announce their decision.

Mayor Thomas was leafing through a volume of Charles Tupper's speeches in the legislative library when the Sergeant-at-Arms found him and said, *"They've asked me to bring you back into the Chamber, sir, to receive your reprimand."*

Reprimand! Mayor Thomas's mood darkened. He had not come all the way to Halifax to be reprimanded for doing what he believed was right and just—and by a bunch of Liberals at that! He refused to return to the Legislative Chamber. His refusal was conveyed to the premier. A few minutes later, the sergeant-at-arms was back with another message:

I must ask you to come with me, Mr. Thomas. I have been ordered to take you into custody on a charge of contempt of the House of Assembly.

With a firm grip on the flabbergasted mayor's arm, he escorted him to the basement, and a barred jail cell. Thomas was summarily pushed inside, the lock secured, and a guard posted nearby, while the sergeant-at-arms went to get the police. David Thomas's fury was unconcealed.

Because of a law that had been passed several years earlier, the premier and his colleagues believed they were completely within their rights to hold Mayor Thomas in custody for up to forty-eight hours.

The sergeant-at-arms hurried over to the new City Hall, where the police station occupied the lower level, and entered the building on the Duke Street side. He went directly to Chief Garret Cotter's office with instructions from the premier that Cotter was to send officers to Province House to take an unruly individual into custody. Detective Nicholas Power and two uniformed officers accompanied the sergeant-at-arms back to Province House.

The cell in the basement of Province House had a cot, a covered pail for personal use in the corner, and just enough room for Thomas to pace, if he chose to do so. It was a mere storage room most of the time, although on rare occasions—prior to Thomas's arrival—it had been used to house criminals. Years earlier, for example, Smith D. Clarke, the convicted murderer of James Bossom, was held there pending his scheduled execution.

As angry as Thomas was already, the sight of uniformed police officers approaching the cell was the last straw. All the way up the basement stairs and out through the main entrance onto Hollis Street, Mayor Thomas vented his anger at the policemen, the sergeant-at-arms, the premier, and every member of the legislature that he happened to meet along the way. He struggled with his irons all the way along George and Barrington Streets to the police station. It would have been a humiliating exercise for most, but Thomas was beyond caring what anyone thought of him. This was an abuse of authority, he screamed to anyone who would listen. Before he was through, he promised, all voting men would know what kind of government they had elected. On and on he went, drawing clusters of curious onlookers as he passed, in the clutches of two burly constables.

Once inside the police station, Thomas soon found himself in a concrete cell much narrower than the one he had just left. The barred door clanged shut behind him, Detective Power and the constables went back to their duties, and the jailer, a Mr. Chambers, took the full brunt of Thomas's verbal outrage. At this stage, any person acting in compliance with the premier's orders was fair game.

Before the day was out, a friend of Thomas's who had witnessed the commotion on the street consulted a lawyer friend, who approached members of the Supreme Court. This was, after all, an exceptional occurrence, and was Thomas really—as he was purported to be—guilty of contempt? The court was quickly convened and, in a matter of hours, ordered the mayor's release on the grounds that the premier and his colleagues were mistaken in their interpretation of the law. Thomas did not complete his full forty-eight hour sentence.

If he thought this would end the matter, Premier Fielding was mistaken. Mayor David Thomas wasted little time in seeking legal advice, and within days launched a lawsuit against the premier, every member of his cabinet, the Liberal caucus, the sergeant-at-arms, the police chief, Detective Power, the two constables, and even Chambers the jailer, asking for damages in the amount of fifty thousand dollars for assault and imprisonment.

Things did not go quite as he hoped, however. In 1895, after weighing every bit of evidence, the Supreme Court did decide in the mayor's favour; but his award was two hundred dollars (six months' salary for a factory worker) payable only by the premier and his caucus.

During the election of 1894, Mayor Thomas made certain the people of Truro remembered this incident and took some satisfaction in Frederick Laurence's subsequent loss. But for the very conservative Mayor Thomas it was a small victory at best, as Premier Fielding's Liberal government was victorious once again. In fact, the Liberals remained in power well past Fielding's retirement.

Though he remained a diehard partisan for the rest of his days, within a few years of his unfortunate incarceration, David J. Thomas gave up on public office and concentrated on running his business.

Frederick Laurence, however, did not retire from politics. He ran for office again in the provincial election of 1897, and handily won his seat. In 1904, he was elected to the parliament of Canada, where he gained a reputation as an astute and dedicated parliamentarian. In 1907, he was appointed a judge of the Superior Court of Nova Scotia.

Eventually, the provincial and federal governments introduced systems of fair compensation for elected members, thereby preventing other incidents like the one that so riled Truro's Mayor Thomas.

18
THE SUFFRAGETTES

(1895)

A struggle for human rights that stretched over three centuries.

An eighteenth-century woman had no voice in public affairs. Her access to any form of education was almost non-existent and, with few opportunities outside of a domestic environment, she was likely to be entirely dependent upon a male relative for protection. In a rough settlement like Halifax, that protection was sometimes fleeting.

For several years following the arrival of the Cornwallis expedition, disease, hardship, and Louisbourg-inspired Indian attacks claimed the lives of hundreds of Haligonians (close to a thousand during the settlement's first year alone). The loss of a protector presented a challenge to the very survival of the women and children left behind.

Frightened and desperate, many widows remarried in haste or put themselves and, in some cases, their children into service to the garrison or to one of the grand new houses of Argyle Street. Others found themselves at the mercy of brothel keepers who operated along the dingy streets near the Citadel. Some of the most desperate, with small children held tightly in their arms, slipped quietly into the cold waters of Halifax Harbour.

A few years later, thanks to the governor's council, they had another choice—the poorhouse on Spring Garden Road.

In its earliest days, successive governors had run the province with the help of an appointed council of male business and property owners. In 1758, after balking at the notion for several years, Governor Charles Lawrence finally complied with London's orders to replace the council with an elected assembly. However, as the only people eligible to vote were Protestant male property owners, and the only people who could run for office were also Protestant male property owners, the average Nova Scotian saw little change.

Over the next few decades, Halifax merchants grew rich from the business of one war after another. During the time of Edward, Duke of Kent, from 1794 to 1800, they embraced a newfound air of respectability. Most left the grimy streets of the town for large new estates south of the Citadel.

Though male Catholic property owners were eventually permitted to vote, the assembly still operated as it had always done. A few women managed to cast votes in the elections of 1793 and 1806, but that may have been more by accident than by design, and a long time would pass before it was allowed to happen again.

At the turn of the nineteenth century, Halifax was still engaged in the business of war—outfitting Royal Navy ships setting off to do battle with Napoleon's forces. Hundreds of French prisoners were being offloaded at the docks and marched across the peninsula to Melville Island. With the outbreak of the War of 1812, captive Americans soon joined the processions.

The effort to gain the vote for women had been going on for close to a century in Britain and elsewhere. In Nova Scotia, however, even though local newspapers carried detailed reports, few women knew of the international suffrage movement. Most, after all, could not read, and of those that could, all but a few read only those pages that had been approved by their husbands.

Access to education was still denied to women, they were not permitted to sit on juries, and mothers had no right to the custody of their own children. Once married, a woman's money or property passed to her husband. In fact, most women owned nothing.

Purchased in 1827 by a young Joseph Howe, the *Novascotian* newspaper took a great interest in the public affairs of the province and, on its editorial pages, criticized not only the electoral system but members of the assembly as well. In 1835, Howe accused sitting magistrates of corruption and was arrested and put on trial. After being acquitted of libel, he returned to his effort to bring about responsible government.

A few months later, on July 29, 1835, an editorial attributed to him entitled "Petticoat Government" (a term coined in Britain a hundred years earlier to describe the absurdity of women voting or holding office) appeared in the *Novascotian*. It read in part:

> *So far as we are concerned, we would willingly consent that the women should assume the government of the world for the next hundred years—and that all mankind should submit to be protected and controlled by such laws as they should in their wisdom enact. The self-styled Lords of the creation have tried their hands at the business long enough in all conscience—they have governed the world for about six centuries—and a precious business they have made of it. The women could do no worse and we shrewdly suspect they could do a great deal better. There is a natural love of order about women that if carried as it assuredly would be into all the*

arrangements of government, could not fail to be productive of the happiest results...

Responsible government became a reality in 1848 with the election of the Liberal government of William Young. In 1854, a new law extended voting privileges to all Nova Scotia men and, while not expressly excluding women, neither did it include them. Joseph Howe was a member of that government, and though in his younger days he may have championed the vote for women, in the 1850s the building of a railroad was his priority.

By the 1880s, girls of upper-class families had access to much more formal education than had their mothers or grandmothers. As a result, a newly confident group of young women began to make their voices heard and, through them, an effort to secure the right to vote gained steam. There was some success in 1887, when Nova Scotia women won the right to vote in municipal elections—provided they were widows or spinsters and owned property—and the women's vote became the subject of serious debate.

In 1893, however, a bill calling for universal suffrage for women was defeated in the Nova Scotia House of Assembly. In 1897, a second bill to extend the franchise to women was defeated as well, but this time by only one vote. The holdout, Attorney General J. W. Longley, justified his position by explaining a woman's role in life:

> *...first, the bearing and bringing up of children. Second, the creating of home and the beautifying of home life...Third, to charm men and make the world pleasant, sweet and agreeable to live in. Fourth, to be kindly and loving, to be sweet and to be cherished, to be weak and confiding, to be protected and to be the object of man's devotion.*

His words did nothing to deter the movement.

The effort to secure women's suffrage was led by women like Edith Jessie Archibald, president of the Women's Christian Temperance Union. She was joined by her cousin, Agnes Dennis, who succeeded her as president of the Local Women's Council in 1906. Along with women like Anna Leonowens, founder of the Victoria School of Art (Nova Scotia College of Art and Design), and Eliza Ritchie, a professor of philosophy at Dalhousie University, the Women's Council took on a number of charitable concerns and actively lobbied for social change.

Through their good works, these women attracted the attention of property developer and philanthropist George Henry Wright. In March 1912, Wright was in England, where he wrote his last will and testament. To the Women's Council of Halifax, he left his home on the corner of Young Avenue and Inglis Street, *"to be used as an institution for carrying on their work and assist in suppressing other evils."* In April, Wright embarked for North America aboard a new ocean liner, the *Titanic.* His body was never recovered.

Early in the twentieth century, the international press was filled with stories—some real, some pure propaganda—of the British suffragettes led by Emmeline Pankhurst, though setting off bombs,or going on hunger strikes to the point of being force-fed were not even considered by Edith Archibald and her colleagues.

Just one of the prominent opposing voices belonged to Reverand John Forrest, former president of Dalhousie University. At the closing exercises of the Halifax Ladies' College on June 17, 1914, he denounced the tactics of militant suffragettes and implored the young ladies present, *"Girls do not, oh do not be suffragettes! Don't be masculine women."* Reverand Forrest believed women's suffrage would ruin civilized society.

Within weeks, however, events in Europe would overtake his concerns. Life would change forever with the outbreak of the First

World War. Edith Archibald, then vice-president of the Nova Scotia Red Cross, was chosen to chair the department responsible for Canadian prisoners of war overseas.

Through the war effort and countless acts of charity, the Women's Council began to earn the respect and admiration of many of their former foes, and in June 1917 they formed the Halifax Suffrage Club to once again lobby politicians. When tragedy struck in December, however, they turned their energies toward a relief effort for victims of the Halifax Explosion, which caused even their most ardent opponents to take notice.

On April 26, 1918, the Liberal government of George Murray passed the *Nova Scotia Franchise Act*, giving Nova Scotia women the same right of participation in provincial elections as men. A month later, women were granted the right to vote in federal elections. In both cases, the competence shown by women during the First World War was cited as justification for the change. The law didn't apply to Aboriginal women, however, who gained the right to vote (along with Aboriginal men) in 1948, though it came with conditions attached. They achieved full and equal rights in 1960.

In 1962, Conservative Gladys Porter of Kings North became the first woman elected to the Nova Scotia House of Assembly.

There was still the matter of equal rights, however. Among other things, the minimum wage was lower for women than men; companies were not required to provide pension plans for their female staff (on the assumption that a woman would always have a man to look after her); and domestic violence, sexual assaults, and gender discrimination were not taken as seriously as they are today.

In the 1960s, building on a foundation created by the suffragettes, an international women's movement began the fight for change, and, though there is still work to be done, particularly on the issue of equal pay for equal work, women today enjoy rights and privileges that earlier generations would never have believed possible.

19

THE BEST DEFENCE

(1900)

A keen wit and a brilliant legal mind.

In the late nineteenth century, the Dalhousie Law School occupied rooms on the second floor of the north wing of the Forrest Building in Halifax, which today sits directly across from the Sir Charles Tupper Medical Building. While the school was able to boast of many accomplished early graduates, few could compare with a brilliant and gregarious young man who hailed from Pictou County.

As a teenager, Jim Maddin was taken on as a machinist's apprentice at the Intercolonial Coal Mine and had no intention of ever moving beyond his small home town. Then, out of the blue, his family was in crisis, and Jim's life took a dramatic turn.

One summer afternoon, his little brother Oliver and one of his friends discovered and began playing with a handgun. The gun suddenly went off, and in a heartbreaking instant the other boy lay dead. Even though several witnesses insisted that it was a dreadful accident, an overzealous sheriff placed young Oliver under arrest and charged him with murder. To his parents' absolute horror, the boy was held in jail for five months before the Grand Jury finally met and released him.

This incident caused Jim to reflect seriously on his own future. If this could happen to an innocent boy like Oliver, he wondered, how many others were in similar or worse situations? So, he announced to the family that he had decided to become a defence attorney and to ensure he had the academic requirements to enter Dalhousie Law School, he resumed his studies at Pictou Academy. At the same time, he took on as many odd jobs as he could find until he had saved enough to cover his tuition.

As he began his studies at Dalhousie Law School, Jim was brimming over with excitement and an eagerness to learn. That, together with an engaging personality, soon made him popular with classmates and faculty alike. As he loved and missed his family, however, he tried to get home to Pictou County to see them whenever he could. It was during one of those visits that he met his future wife, Maude, and, by the time he graduated in 1900, the couple were married and had two children.

Jim's sense of humour was legendary, but sometimes the laugh was on him.

One bright, sunny afternoon, during final exams in his graduating year, he took a break from studying and headed downtown. Along Barrington Street he ran into an old friend from Pictou County who was working aboard a West Indies freighter that had come into port for supplies, and Jim didn't need to be asked twice to accompany the fellow back to the ship for a good chat over a bottle of Jamaican rum. Hours later, vibrations of the ship's engine roused him from a drink-induced sleep. Realizing that the vessel was moving, he ran up to the deck to find that they were steaming past McNab's Island toward the harbour mouth and ultimately, he assumed, to the West Indies. With panicky thoughts of Maude and the children not knowing what had happened to him, as well as of missing the rest of his examinations,

Jim drew on every bit of charm he could muster and convinced the captain to put him ashore. A small boat was lowered and, after being dropped off at an outcropping near Chebucto Head, Jim made the long trek back to Halifax.

Following graduation, Jim was told he would not be accepted to the Bar due to a technicality in his matriculation. Luckily, the president of the Nova Scotia Barristers Society, Robert Borden, had met young Maddin on several occasions and, when he heard of the problem, personally stepped in and helped resolve it.

Jim practiced law at Springhill for a few years before moving to Sydney, and in 1908, changed course again. At the urging of Borden, who was by this time leader of the federal Conservative Party, Jim Maddin ran for and won the seat of Cape Breton South for the Tories—even though at heart he was a Liberal. He quite enjoyed his experience as a Member of Parliament, and in the next election, in 1911, he returned to his Liberal roots. Unfortunately, the Liberal Party was trounced, as was he, and his former colleagues formed the government, with his old friend Borden now the prime minister.

At the outbreak of the First World War, every young man in the country was keen to do his part and Jim was no exception. Leaving Maude and the children in Sydney, he headed to Halifax to enlist in the 85th Overseas Battalion, CEF, as a captain. Within months, he was promoted to major.

As responsible and professional as he was when on duty, Jim's sense of humour and good fun was never far from the surface. While on leave in London, he and a number of friends spent much of an evening drinking at the Savoy Hotel and, late that night, emerged slightly worse for wear onto the darkened Strand. London was in blackout. Now, every soldier at the time was issued a whistle, which was to be blown only in cases of emergency. Frivolous use could result in court martial. Even so, as he emerged into the night, Jim told friends later, he was overcome by the urge to blow his whistle and gave it *"a hell of a blast."*

Suddenly, out of the darkness came a handful of London bobbies and their senior officer demanded to know who had raised the alarm and why. Jim knew he had to come up with something, and fast. He assumed his most authoritative posture and ordered the man to round up all the policemen he could find and bring them to him on the double. The young policeman had no interest in upsetting an officer, so he sent two men off in search of others. In no time at all, about a dozen more policemen emerged from the darkness.

Jim recalled reading in the newspaper earlier in the day that the lord mayor was hosting an important conference and so he told the bobbies that he was under orders to test the efficiency of the security forces within the city. He ordered them into formation and for several minutes drilled and inspected them right there on the Strand before commending and dismissing them with the lord mayor's thanks. Within the hour, however, the senior police officer caught up with Jim and his friends. Realizing they had been tricked, but too embarrassed to file a report, the young man promised not to arrest Jim for sounding the alarm, if he in turn agreed not to tell police superiors what had happened.

After the war, Jim returned to Sydney, resumed his practice, and, with success after success, became known as one of the country's most skilful trial lawyers. In over sixty murder cases, only two of his clients met the executioner.

This proud son of an Irish father and Scottish mother was easily recognizable even to those who knew him only by reputation. He was rarely without his trademark green tie, almost never wore socks (even in the dead of winter), and, though he dealt in the seriousness of criminal law, he was warm and funny enough to earn the adoration of his children, his grandchildren, and his neighbours.

Whether defending a murderer or lecturing on any number of topics, Jim Maddin was such a charismatic orator that people would travel miles just to hear him speak.

His speaking skills served him well in a dangerous situation in the summer of 1919. He, Sydney's chief of police, and the crown prosecutor set out together in search of an armed fugitive named Grant who was being sought in connection with a murder. At the outskirts of town they spotted Grant in a farm field and, though the man had a loaded revolver, Jim walked out to speak with him. Thinking he was mad to do so, the chief of police and crown prosecutor stayed well back. In a matter of minutes, however, Grant willingly gave up his weapon, walked out of the field alongside Jim, and surrendered to police.

Months later Hollywood came to town and, for a lark, Jim charmed his way into roles in two of the first moving pictures shot in Cape Breton—*Clansmen of the North* and *Sea Riders*—though even he had to admit that he was a better lawyer than actor.

In 1954, eighty-year-old Jim Maddin chose to slow down just slightly by taking on the role of stipendiary magistrate for Sydney, and for the rest of his days he continued to act in the best interests of family, friends, and his community.

The *Chronicle Herald* reported on Saturday, September 30, 1961: "*Major 'Jim' Maddin, 87, one of Canada's most colourful courtroom personalities, died Friday…his passing lowered the final curtain on a life dedicated to the legal profession.*"

20
TITANIC HALIGONIANS

(1912)

There were two Haligonians on the Titanic;
one survived, the other did not.

Hilda Mary Slayter was the daughter of a prominent Halifax family. Her father, Dr. William Bruce Slayter, was not only a well-respected physician but an accomplished tenor as well, and Hilda had inherited his gift for music. She had a fine voice and was much in demand at church socials, but she wanted so much more. At the age of twenty, in 1902, Hilda travelled to Italy, where she hoped that she might one day become a professional singer. With her family's support, she was able to study and live in Italy for seven years, before coming to the realization that her dreams would never be fulfilled.

On a visit with Canadian friends, she was introduced to Reginald Lacon, the son of a British nobleman who, at the time, had a home on Denman Island off the coast of British Columbia. The relationship blossomed and by 1912, the young couple was planning to marry. To ensure she had the best possible trousseau, Hilda sailed to England to do her shopping, booking her return voyage aboard a luxurious new ocean liner.

With trunks carrying her wedding gown and trousseau safely checked in, Hilda boarded the *Titanic* at Queenstown, Ireland, and moved into a second-class cabin with a Londoner named Florence Kelly. A few nights later, when disaster struck, both were able to get safely into separate lifeboats and were eventually brought aboard the *Carpathia* and taken to New York City. On June 1, Mary and Reginald Lacon were married on Denman Island. They had a son, also called Reginald, who became a decorated hero of the Second World War, and Mary spent her widowhood at his home on the Isle of Wight. After she died there in 1965, she was returned to Halifax for burial at Camp Hill Cemetery.

George Wright was born in 1849 on a farm near Tufts Cove, Dartmouth, but his interest was in business, not farming. During a visit to Philadelphia at the age of twenty-seven, George recognized the need for an international business directory, and soon set himself up in the publishing trade. Before long, Wright's Business Directories were being published for most of the world's major cities, and by the time he was thirty, George Wright was a wealthy man.

In the 1890s, he was back in Halifax. He joined the Royal Halifax Yacht Club (now the Royal Nova Scotia Yacht Squadron), where he sailed two yachts of his own, and travelled in the best social circles. The Wright Trophy is still being awarded annually in his memory.

Now that he was back home, George decided to invest in property development and soon formed a business partnership with a well-respected architect, James Dumaresq. Together they designed and built several office buildings, two of which—the St. Paul's Building at the corner of Prince Street and the Marble Building a few doors south—are still standing. In 1902, Wright had Dumaresq design and build a private residence for him at the corner of Young Avenue and Inglis Street.

But George was much more than a property developer or publisher. He was, in fact, a man well ahead of his time. He had a strong social conscience, and became a benefactor to countless charities. For example, he and Dumaresq came up with an idea for the first mixed-income housing development in Halifax. Starting at the north end of Holy Cross Cemetery on South Park Street and running right up to Morris Street, they built grand homes for the wealthy. Then, for one block along Morris, there were homes destined for middle-class families. The Morris Street development led straight to Wright Court (now Wright Avenue), where they built homes that would provide comfort to working-class families—many of whom were employed as servants in the grander homes on South Park Street.

George Wright embraced many causes. He lectured and wrote newspaper articles on the evils of strong drink, prostitution, and the abject poverty that society expected widows and children to endure. But it wasn't just words. George generously donated one of his properties to a women's group, for use as a shelter for homeless women and children.

Proving time and again that he was a man ahead of his time, George Wright also supported the work of the suffragettes (as mentioned in Chapter 18). Whenever the suffragettes required meeting space, he would provide rooms in one of his buildings.

In the spring of 1912, coming home from a business trip to England, Wright bought a first-class ticket for the maiden voyage of a luxurious new liner, the *Titanic*. When disaster struck, it is believed that George—who was a very heavy sleeper—likely slept through the warnings until it was too late to escape. His body was never recovered.

As he never married, his friends and acquaintances had long ago concluded that George was gay. Within weeks of the disaster, his lawyers notified his heirs about the contents of his will, in which Halifax's Council of Women inherited his house.

He left another $226,000 to various charities, along with $20,000 to the City of Halifax for a building to *"to check the lure and bad influences of the streets."* By 1951, this fund had grown, with interest, to over $80,000, and the city had yet to decide what to do with it. Finally, the decision was left to the Supreme Court and as a result, the money was used to construct the YMCA building on South Park Street.

Though George's body was never recovered and he has no final resting place in Halifax, his family erected a tombstone in his memory in a Dartmouth cemetery, and it just takes a walk around town to know that he is still a part of this community.

21

DEADMAN'S ISLAND

(1920)

A soldier's grave is shrouded in mystery.

In the 1920s a rumour began circulating in Halifax that there was buried treasure on a peninsula that jutted out from the western shore of the Northwest Arm.

Known in the early nineteenth century as Target Hill, the place was used by the admiralty throughout the Napoleonic Wars and the War of 1812 as a burial ground for hundreds of prisoners of war from nearby Melville Island. French, Spanish, Italian, and American bones lay deep in its rocky soil. While some had been claimed by disease and others by accidents, murder, or suicide, all were quickly and quietly disposed of with little or no observance to their passing.

Target Hill was so named because it was where soldiers of the guard held regular target practice, amid the graves of hundreds of young men not unlike themselves.

In the years that followed the wars, the Melville Island Fever Hospital took the place of the prison, and within its walls hundreds of men, women, and children suffering from contagious diseases—escaped slaves and Welsh immigrants among them—died from their infections and were buried alongside the dead soldiers of Target Hill. Any markers that were placed over these dead have not stood the passage of time.

In the spring of 1819, a gradual erosion of the shoreline had begun to disturb the resting place of Melville's dead and two men laying traps near Target Hill were alarmed by the sight of an exposed human skull. Over the next several months, other people came forward with their own discoveries and before long locals had dubbed the place "Deadman's Island." The burials, however, were not yet over.

The admiralty still owned Melville Island, and in the 1840s once again authorized its use as a quarantine station, this time to house Irish immigrants from ships infected with smallpox. Within days of the immigrants' arrival, a long-practiced ritual resumed and, once again, shrouded bodies were being transported after dark to Deadman's Island for speedy burial.

It is impossible to say precisely how many graves there are on Deadman's Island, although records indicate that there were approximately 195 Americans, 75 to 100 French, Spaniards, and Italians, 104 former slaves, and dozens of Welsh and Irish immigrants laid to rest in its soil.

The history of the island isn't entirely tragic, however. For about twenty years in the late nineteenth century, Deadman's Island was a popular fairground. Among the unmarked graves there were such attrations as a scenic railway, a theatre, shooting galleries, a dance hall, and ice cream booths. The owner was a well-liked Irish entrepreneur named Longley and, as much as he tried to deny it, every now and then Longley came into contact with the island's dark side. Once, while preparing a berry patch, he accidentally unearthed three human skulls. He promptly placed them in the rafters of the dance hall's basement as a deterrent to people wandering down there. Unfortunately, it was no deterrent at all. Not only did people still go down there, the skulls were stolen.

Among the hundreds of graves, however, there is one that for more than a century has been steeped in mystery and romance. It is believed to be the last resting place of a tragic young soldier— Private John Dixon of Sydney, Cape Breton. Dixon, so the legend goes, was a handsome young man of a good family who, within a few months of joining the 63rd Regiment, was posted as an orderly to the home of its colonel. There, he met and fell hopelessly in love with the officer's eighteen-year-old daughter; and though for several months the young lovers met secretly, their relationship eventually came to the colonel's attention. In a rage, he sent young Dixon back to the 63rd, and forbade his daughter from ever seeing him again.

Shortly after, with a trumped-up charge of theft against him, Dixon was tried by court martial and confined to Melville Island, which by this time had become a military prison. His distraught friends later claimed that the young man was in such distress over the loss of his true love that one day, overcome by melancholy, he simply walked away from the prison yard and into the waters of Melville Cove to drown. Following protocol, members of the guard buried him late at night on Deadman's Island, then constructed a memorial around their friend's grave. In the decades that followed, successive generations of Melville's soldiers faithfully cared for the site.

In the early twentieth century, the story of Deadman's Island took yet another turn. A rumour began to spread in Halifax that, rather than a body, the grave of Private John Dixon held buried treasure. This went on for several months, until one night several young fellows decided to see for themselves. Under cover of darkness and armed with picks and shovels, they made their way to the foot of Jubilee Road, borrowed a small boat that was beached nearby, and rowed across the Arm.

They spent the next hour or so digging into the rocky soil, only to find that buried beneath the grave surface was—a large pile of rocks! No body. No treasure.

A mystery remains. Who was John Dixon? And why did several generations of soldiers so faithfully tend his grave?

22
MACHINE GUN KELLY

(1920–1935)

*At the sound of gunfire, the smugglers knew
precisely who was following them.*

For more than 150 years, in a space considerably smaller than a square mile, hundreds of Halifax grog shops, alehouses, and taverns did a roaring trade off the king's men and locals alike. As a result, alcoholism was rampant throughout the town—from the mean streets of The Hill to the finer neighbourhoods to the south—even among children as young as ten years of age.

Drink-induced robberies, criminal assaults, and even some murders kept the police busy around the clock, and in an age when social programs were non-existent, the human toll was almost overwhelming. Beginning in the middle of the nineteenth century, local clergy began following the lead of their British counterparts and forming temperance societies that advocated against the sale and consumption of alcohol of any kind. In a town that seemed to run on rum, it was an uphill battle.

The problem wasn't unique to Nova Scotia. All across Canada and in the United States, temperance movements were formed under the leadership of Methodists, Presbyterians, and Congregationalists. No matter how hard they worked or how firm their resolve, however, they saw very little in the way of success.

At the turn of the twentieth century, things began to change. Prince Edward Island established prohibition in 1901, and gradually, over the duration of the First World War, the other provinces and territories, with the exception of Quebec and British Columbia, followed suit. This led, in the 1920s, to a marked decrease in certain types of crimes. However, it also spawned a new criminal industry. Underground taverns, known as "speakeasies" or "blind pigs," began to spring up from one end of Nova Scotia to the other.

There were exceptions to the prohibition rule, however. With a doctor's note, an "ill" Nova Scotian could go to a pharmacy to purchase liquor for "medicinal purposes." The Halifax police noticed, however, that around Christmas there seemed to be an inordinate number of "sick" people lining up at pharmacies all over town.

On January 16, 1919, the Eighteenth Amendment to the Constitution of the United States established prohibition of the "manufacture, sale, or transportation of intoxicating liquors within, the importation thereof into, or the exportation thereof from the United States." And a new and very lucrative industry was spawned all along the Atlantic coast of Canada. Rum-running.

All through the 1920s and early 1930s, French and British cargo ships delivered thousands of bottles of whiskey, wine, brandy, and other fine spirits to the tiny islands of St. Pierre et Miquelon, where fishermen from Nova Scotia and Newfoundland were waiting. From there, the cargo was transferred to the holds of Newfoundland and Nova Scotian fishing boats. And the fishermen set off for one of a select few coves, where the booze was stored until a larger, faster ship, owned by an American syndicate, collected and delivered it to the United States.

The smuggling of contraband liquor into the United States was dangerous work, but it was also the stuff that adventures are made of. There was no shortage of young fishermen willing to sign up, when an enterprising ship owner came calling. For their part, hundreds of young Canadians saw the trip to exotic St. Pierre—with its beautiful girls and free-flowing wine—as a bonus. After the depression hit in 1929, money was tight, jobs were scarce, and smuggling increased dramatically.

At times, entire communities were aware of what was going on and quietly looked the other way. These men, after all, were neighbours, who were merely providing for their families the best they could. In the village of Prospect, for example, even the parish priest got involved. The basement of Our Lady of Mount Carmel Glebe House, which sat right on the edge of the bay, was used to store contraband liquor. Another particularly successful base of operations throughout the 1920s and early 1930s was near Digby on the Bay of Fundy—aptly named Smuggler's Cove. Here, as in Prospect, home owners along the shore hired their cellars and sheds out for storage.

While the prohibition era increased certain types of criminal activity in Canada, in the United States it gave birth to a virtual wave of organized crime and involved notorious figures like Al Capone, Dutch Shultz, and a mobster that went by the name of Machine Gun Kelly.

Strangely enough, Nova Scotia had its own "Machine Gun Kelly." He wasn't a mobster, however. He was a cop!

An affable, outgoing fellow, Captain J. C. Kelly of the Customs Department took great pride in his work. In fact, it's fair to say that he loved it. As a part of the marine division of the RCMP, Kelly patrolled the Bay of Fundy all through the prohibition years, hunting down and sometimes capturing would-be smugglers. In an interview with host Don Tremaine on CBC Radio in 1970, Kelly explained that on the Canadian side of the border the relationship between law enforcement and smugglers was, for the most part, collegial. Each side had a job to do, and did it to the best of its abilities.

For the smugglers, it was a great way to make money—and to get all the free booze they could drink. Though there were some independent contractors, for the most part ships were hired and owned by American syndicates. It wasn't difficult to find men to crew these ships, as the pay was considerably higher than on a fishing boat.

While, for the most part, the men were paid very well, the syndicate owners made a fortune. A single cargo of liquor, for example, could fetch as much as $100,000 (equal to about $1.3 million in 2012) on the American side of the bay. And when any of their men were caught, the syndicate would simply underwrite their $1,000 ($13,000 in 2012 dollars) as one of the costs of doing business. Nova Scotia fishermen did very well also, by hiring their boats out to the syndicates and earning considerably more from a load of liquor than they would from a load of fish.

Kelly got the nickname "Machine Gun" because of the weapon mounted on the bow of his patrol boat—a weapon he formally requisitioned and was surprised to see delivered. Whenever his patrol boat approached a suspected rum-runner, he'd call out, *"Heave to in the name of the king!"* And if that didn't get results, he'd fire a few warning rounds from the machine gun. Eventually, all he had to do was fire off a few rounds for a vessel to know who was approaching.

Despite a constant RCMP patrol on the Bay of Fundy, no more than ten percent of the rum-runners were ever caught. Why? Because the syndicates had the money to buy bigger and faster boats. The RCMP did not. Kelly noted that even chasing the rum-runners on land was a challenge. They had cars, while most of the time the Mounties were on horseback.

With the exception of PEI, prohibition ended in Canada in 1930, and many of the speakeasies and blind pigs along Halifax's

Water and Brunswick Streets were converted into legitimate taverns. Prohibition in the United States continued for a few more years, however, and business continued to be brisk across the Bay of Fundy. In the early thirties, the RCMP patrol boats were supplemented by RCAF air patrols, but the capture rate remained about the same.

The era that brought widespread corruption and organized crime to American cities, and made legends out of the likes of Al Capone and Dutch Schultz, came to an end in 1934. Until the end of their days, though, Nova Scotia's rum-runners fondly remembered the most interesting and adventurous time of their lives.

23

MARY ELLEN'S GHOST

(1922)

An Antigonish tale of terror.

In early 1922, a mystery was brewing on a small farm in Caledonia Mills, Antigonish County. In a matter of days, what appeared to be a ghostly presence drove the MacDonald family out of their home and within weeks, the incident was being reported in newspapers all around the world.

It had been Alexander MacDonald's habit to rise early and go downstairs to light the kitchen fire before waking his wife and their fifteen-year-old adopted daughter, Mary Ellen. The morning of Friday, January 6, was like any other, until Alexander reached the kitchen and found ashes on the stove top and a scorched ceiling overhead. Suddenly, in the next room an armchair burst into flame and, following that, a sofa. Alexander rushed to get the burning furniture outside and doused the flames with snow.

He took a careful look around and assured himself that the house was safe once again and, though he couldn't explain the fires, he was not overly concerned. With kerosene lanterns, wood stoves, and fireplaces still in regular use on many small farms, fires were not all that uncommon. Surely, he thought, there was a logical explanation. That evening, after the family's evening meal, with the stove fire extinguished, he did another more thorough search of the place and convinced himself that there would be no more problems.

Several hours later, however, Mrs. MacDonald awoke in a panic. She could smell smoke! The wall and floorboards surrounding the kitchen chimney were ablaze, and though Alexander was able to quickly put the flames out, a few minutes later the fire started again.

The following Sunday night, the same thing happened, only now the family was living in a state of fear. Alexander put out the fire, and Mrs. MacDonald and Mary Ellen went to bed—the only way to stay warm in the icy cold house. Alexander, on the other hand, remained downstairs in deep thought, trying to figure out what was happening. But he wasn't able to think long, because a second fire broke out in the ceiling overhead, and no sooner had that been extinguished, but three others followed in quick succession. Alexander was at his wits' end.

Monday passed without any further occurrences, and the family fell exhausted into their beds that night. But late Tuesday afternoon the trouble started again. Alexander was out in the barn when the wallpaper in the dining room began to burn. It was quickly doused by Mrs. MacDonald and Mary Ellen, but other fires began breaking out—one in a pile of rags upstairs, others on wallpaper throughout the house. In a panic, Mrs. MacDonald and Mary Ellen ran to their nearest neighbours for help.

Leo and Dan McGillivray, along with Duncan McDonald, lived about a half mile away and, seeing the women's obvious distress, returned to the MacDonald farm with them. At the house, they found Alexander in terrible state. He was frightened, confused, and exhausted. He had just put out three more fires. As all seemed calm for the moment, everyone gathered in the small kitchen and, because it was so cold, tentatively lit a fire in the stove.

They had no sooner begun to relax when a bright light lit up the main living and dining room. Leo McGillivray ran into that room, pulled a burning shade down from the window, and stomped it out. Over the rest of that day and throughout the night, there were thirty more eruptions in the strangest of places…on wallpaper, behind pictures, in cushions—even a cloth lying in a pool of water lit up.

But the mystery wasn't confined to the MacDonalds' home. Peculiar things were also happening in the barn. A few days before the fires started, Alexander had begun to find his cows and horses in a state of advanced distress at all hours. Cows and horses were moved about the barn and found in different stalls, their tails braided. On one occasion, all of the animals were locked outside the barn and at least once, Alexander found his horses inexplicably lathered in sweat in the middle of the night.

On January 12, Alexander had had enough. Believing that the fires would ultimately consume the entire house, and with the lives of his family at stake, he accepted the McGillivrays' invitation to stay with them for an extended period of time. In the days and weeks that followed, Alexander returned to the farm to care for his livestock, but he avoided going into the house.

Now, the MacDonalds were a good family, known to be God-fearing and generous of spirit. As the story of their experiences spread about the county, those who knew them believed this had to be a supernatural occurrence.

As witnesses such as the McGillivrays were quick to point out, the house was tiny and it would have been virtually impossible for a family member, or even for a visitor to carry out these terrifying deeds undiscovered. On the ground floor there was only the main room—a living and dining area—of twenty-two by twenty-six feet, with a small kitchen off one end. Upstairs, under a pitched roof, was the only bedroom.

The events in Caledonia Mills soon reached the ears of the editor of the *Halifax Herald*, who sent reporter Harold B. Whidden—in the company of police detective Peter Owen Carroll—to Caledonia Mills to investigate. These two middle-aged men were known to be sensible, and not in the least possessed by overactive imaginations.

On February 15, in the company of Alexander MacDonald, they spent the night in the farmhouse in the hope of seeing for themselves what was really going on. All three slept in the same room. Nothing happened. The next night, however, Whidden and Carroll had the frights of their lives. They heard strange sounds, they said, and felt the touch of an unseen hand (both claimed to have been slapped). Alexander MacDonald saw and heard nothing.

Back in Halifax, Whidden wrote of their experiences for the newspaper, stating unequivocally that he and Carroll were both of the firm belief that the MacDonalds were telling the truth about their haunted house.

When he read Whidden's account, Edward J. O'Brien, a Boston scientist who was lecturing at St. Francis Xavier University, headed to the MacDonald house to look into the matter. A few weeks later, he drew several conclusions. While he didn't doubt that Whidden and Carroll believed they had been struck by a ghost, O'Brien felt the explanation was much simpler. In his opinion, the so-called slaps had merely been reflexive actions of their own arms that were numbed by the extreme cold of the room (twenty-five degrees below zero Celsius).

And, second, there was a scientific reason, he claimed, for the fires as well. Backed up by experts such as the great inventor Guglielmo Marconi himself, O'Brien cited as the cause two radio stations— one in Glace Bay and the other in Massachusetts. The MacDonald house, he said, was situated directly in the path of electrical currents passing between them. The solution was a simple one. The

MacDonalds should move. As for the matter of the livestock, he blamed Mary Ellen and accused her of getting up to mischief.

Newspapers across Canada, the United States, and Britain picked up the story of the Antigonish ghost, and were soon reporting that an eminent "ghost hunter," Dr. Walter F. Prince, of New York, had been invited by Mr. W. H. Dennis, the editor of the *Halifax Herald*, to carry out an investigation of his own. Dr. Prince was a prominent officer of the American Institute of Scientific Research. In reporting his involvement, a Michigan newspaper advised its readers, *"It must be borne in mind that Nova Scotia is 'wet territory' and ghosts inhabit wet places."*

While Dr. Prince was carrying out his research, complete with ghost traps and the jingling of bells, Harold Whidden returned to interview him, and took part in an experiment involving automatic writing. Whidden was given a pencil, and, in a hypnotic state, became a means of communicating with the spirit world. While much of what he wrote was not useful, Whidden claimed that a spirit did guide his hand, so aggressively at times that several pencils were broken in the process. He later reported that it had been a disturbing experience that left him confused and dazed for several hours after. He also claimed to have written a fuller report of his automatic writing experience—in detail that would have been too disturbing for the general public to read—and filed it away for future reference.

In March, Dr. Prince published his report—"An Investigation of Poltergeist and Other Phenomena near Antigonish"—and based his findings on a one-week stay in the house. Prince dismissed eyewitness accounts as errors in judgment, and gave no credence to the claims of Harold Whidden or Detective Carroll. He believed the noises they heard were caused by the wind, and that the slaps they both claimed to have experienced were products of their imaginations. As for the automatic writing experiment, he remained unconvinced.

He made light of O'Brien's electrical-current theory, and placed the entire blame for the fires and the livestock incidents on the daughter, Mary Ellen.

Dr. Prince's report was met with skepticism by most Nova Scotians, especially those in Antigonish, who believed that it was absurd to blame Mary Ellen. In fact, they took offence at Dr. Prince's description of her as being of limited intelligence and frequently in a dreamlike state. To those who knew her, she was nothing like that. Rather, she was a bright, kind young lady who was devoted to her parents and would never cause them such distress. Prince clarified his point by saying that Mary Ellen was in such a deficient mental state that she would not have been aware of what she was doing.

Even the famous author Sir Arthur Conan Doyle got into the act. Happening to be visiting Canada at the time, he argued that Mary Ellen could very well have been the medium of the ghost of *"some naughty boy, whom not even death could cure of his mischievousness."*

The people of Antigonish were unconvinced.

Poor Mary Ellen MacDonald. She was being described around the world as a simple girl who set fires and tortured livestock. She and her parents were so angry with Dr. Prince's accusations that they remained in seclusion at the McGillivrays' for months while a media storm grew around them. The elder MacDonalds, both in their seventies, would hear nothing against Mary Ellen and welcomed the support of family and friends. In October, a New York newspaper reported that she had been committed to an insane asylum, after being caught setting a fire in the family barn. The interest in the "Mary Ellen Spook" was relentless.

A few years later, Mary Ellen married and left Nova Scotia to live in Ontario. After her departure there were no more reports of fires at the little house in Caledonia Mills.

24

THE HUNT FOR LOUIS BEVIS

(1924)

*Haligonians dodge bullets as a posse races
through the city.*

On Saturday morning, July 12, 1924, four young Haligonians made a decision that would change their lives and several others, forever.

At twenty-five, Louis Bevis was the oldest. A war veteran, he had been desperately trying to get steady employment after being court-martialled for theft. His mother, Alice, adored her son, but had several younger children to support after being abandoned by their father years earlier. So, when he suggested going to the States to live with his father, where he was assured of a job, Alice agreed that he could take his thirteen-year-old sister, Muriel, with him—provided he look out for her. She wasn't too concerned about this latest idea of his because she knew that neither he nor his sister had money for their train fare.

A day later, Louis and Muriel met friends Wilfred Slaughenwhite and his fifteen-year-old sister, Ethel, who begged to be allowed to come along. But they didn't have any money either, and Louis came up with what he thought was a brilliant idea.

Over the previous few months, Halifax had been experiencing a crime wave of sorts. Burglaries were at an all-time high, and newspapers rarely missed an opportunity to criticize the mayor and the chief of police for their apparent inability to put a stop to it. Louis concluded that one more burglary wouldn't make a lot of difference.

Wilfred and the girls disagreed at first, but Louis could be persuasive and explained that he knew just the house. The owners were away, it was near the Arm and fairly isolated, and they should be able to get in and out without being seen. The house was Coburg Cottage, where it is believed an early owner, the Pryor family, had displayed Nova Scotia's first Christmas tree. Later, the house had been owned by Sir Sandford Fleming, the inventor of worldwide standard time.

On Sunday morning, after spending the night camping out in the woods, they set out for the cottage. Louis went inside while the others stood watch, and when he emerged, he not only had goods that would raise enough money for train tickets, he proudly displayed another treasure—a handgun and bullets!

Since the pawn shop wouldn't open until Monday morning, they had to spend one more night in the woods. As a precaution, Louis suggested they find a different campsite. After crossing the Arm Bridge they followed a path along the west side and at first chose a site that was on private land.

When the owner, Frank Longard, spotted them and tried to chase them off, Louis foolishly waved the gun to scare him. Longard called the police, of course, and in what seemed no time at all, several police cars with bells sounding were racing down the Herring Cove Road. Dropping their loot but keeping the gun, the four young friends ran into the woods. The boys knew these woods well, and led the girls to a trail that took them toward a church near the head of the Arm. Next morning, they left the church, and seeing no sign of police, hoped that they had lost interest in a "trespassing" complaint. Feeling relatively secure, the four of them headed up the Dutch Village Road until they met a bread wagon from Fry's bakery.

They were hungry, and while Wilfred and the girls hoped to convince the driver to give them some stale bread, Louis had other ideas. Pulling the gun, he robbed the driver of about seven dollars. In all his years of thieving, it had never been so easy to get money.

After pocketing the cash, they continued up the Dutch Village Road and entered a field known as the Fairview Grounds. Being not especially wise thieves, they apparently didn't realize that the bread truck driver would run to get help. After being tipped off by him and by locals who had seen where they had gone, the police were moving in.

When they saw a police car approaching, all four ran toward the new Ashburn Golf Club, leaving the road just opposite its gates and heading across another field and into some trees. With guns drawn, several police officers were close behind. There was an exchange of gunfire, and one of the police officers, Stephen Kennedy, was hit. While Kennedy was being loaded into a car for the journey to hospital, the girls and Wilfred ran off in one direction and Louis in another.

Wilfred, Ethel, and Muriel were soon in custody but Louis was on the run, across town.

Meanwhile, the mayor, already smarting from media criticism over the burglaries, was not going to allow a gun-toting madman to run loose in his city. Every Halifax police officer, an RCMP squad from the dockyard, the Canadian National Railway Police, and members of the Fire Department turned out, and were joined by hundreds of civilians who answered a call for volunteers. According to newspaper reports, upwards of a thousand men—most of them armed with revolvers or rifles—were given orders to *"shoot to kill"* and to bring in the villains *"dead or alive."*

Armed men, most of whom had no idea how to properly handle a gun, swarmed the city. Some headed for Point Pleasant Park, scaring the life out of tourists. Others commandeered cars and spread out over normally quiet neighbourhoods on the hunt for the Bevis gang.

At the same time, Louis was crossing Quinpool Road and heading straight for Preston Street where he stopped at his aunt's house. Knowing nothing of what was going on, she fixed him a sandwich and a glass of milk. It was around four o'clock when word got out that Louis had been spotted on Preston Street. Six or seven motorcars raced to the scene, stopping in front of the house. Several policemen, led by Officer Charles Fulton, leapt from the running boards and closed in on the building with guns drawn. But Louis had seen them coming and ran out the back door and through the yard, where he climbed over a fence in a hail of bullets and was wounded in the heel. His injury was slight and not enough to stop him, so he kept going until he reached the field behind St. Thomas Aquinas School and ran toward a grove of trees at the far end.

People had begun, foolishly, to line the streets to catch a glimpse of the chase. More and more civilian members of the posse arrived, firing haphazardly. One bullet went through a glass front door on LeMarchant Street. Two more went through the living room window of a house on Chestnut Street, hitting the wall at about a foot above the chair where the owner was sitting. Two men painting a house on Jubilee Road ran for cover as bullets whizzed by them; and several war veterans said later that there was so much gunfire, they thought the war had started again and that Halifax was under siege.

Officer Fulton led the chase, and as the posse closed in, Bevis turned and fired two shots, then kept going toward Camp Hill Cemetery. For a moment there was a pause. Fulton lay wounded, and his friends commandeered a car to rush him to hospital where, within minutes of arriving, he was pronounced dead. The police eventually caught up with Bevis, hiding in some bushes near the south end of the cemetery near Carleton Street, and took him into custody. Alice Bevis arrived at the jail a few hours later, in absolute despair over the fate of two of her children.

Within days, the Slaughenwhites were charged with theft, Muriel was sent off to the Maritime Home for Girls in Truro, and Bevis was remanded until the fall sitting of the Supreme Court, charged with the murder of Officer Charles Fulton and the attempted murder of Officer Stephen Kennedy.

Officer Fulton was a well-liked and highly respected young man who was recently married, and had many friends and family. Most people in town knew the Fultons, and none had an unkind word to say about them. Friends, neighbours, and even complete strangers mourned.

This was not lost on Crown Prosecutor O'Hearn, who was also the attorney general and up for re-election. He knew he would never be forgiven if Bevis walked free. He was fairly confident, however, in the evidence and witness testimony.

A defence attorney from Sydney, James W. Maddin, offered his services free of charge to the Bevis family, because he believed the charge should have been manslaughter, not murder.

As it turned out, there were two trials. The first, which began on October 10, ended in a hung jury due to a lack of bullet evidence. The Crown did not present any, as the bullet fragments taken from Fulton's head did not weigh enough to have come from Bevis's gun. While the Crown put this down to the chaos at the time of Fulton's death, both on the field and in the hospital, the jury could not agree. In advance of the second trial, however, a mortician at Snow's Funeral Home came forward with more bullet fragments that had apparently been found during the embalming process and set aside.

At the second trial, which began on November 17, the Crown

called two new witnesses, both from Snow's. The receptionist, Miss Murdoch, and Mr. Clarence Burns, assistant mortician testified that during embalming additional fragments of a bullet had been found, although they had not been turned over to the attorney general until the eve of the second trial. Under cross-examination by Maddin, Burns said that he had not come forward sooner because he had been unaware of the first trial. As the entire town had been caught up in the drama, Maddin said, that was highly unlikely, especially considering that Burns's wife was Louis's aunt and her nephew was on trial for his life.

In his final address, Maddin tried to convince the jury that no murder had been committed. There was, he said, a very tragic accident resulting in the death of a fine young man caused by an overzealous and out-of-control mob. But the jury would have none of it. Louis Bevis, they believed, had started a chain of events that ended in tragedy. Therefore he alone was responsible.

On December 3, 1924, Louis Bevis was sentenced to death.

Of all the victims in this sad tale, however, one was all but forgotten. No matter what he had done, Louis was still his mother's boy. She loved him unconditionally, and was heartbroken over what he had done, and how his life had ended. On the night before his execution he wrote his last letter to her:

Halifax
Midnight, February 10, 1925

Hello my sweet Mother,

Now you be a good Mummy and don't you worry, as all is well, because your precious boy is going to Heaven and he will pray for you there and he will meet you there someday. Now, Mother dear, here is a flower that my lips have kissed.

I am sending it to you so you can say you had the last kiss from your boy's lips. I just had a cup of tea and a piece of pie and I feel great.

Mr. Harding is staying with me all night so bye bye dear Mother of Love, with oceans of love, and a kiss on every wave.

I close for ever more,

Louis

25

MONA AND THE NAZIS

(1939)

A small-town Nova Scotia girl faces death by firing squad.

Mona Louise Parsons was born in 1901 at 370 Main Street, Middleton, in the Annapolis Valley of Nova Scotia. The daughter of a successful local merchant, she was a bright, energetic, and outgoing child who charmed everyone around her. At Acadia University she embraced her passion for acting, taking part in the school's dramatic productions and earning a name for herself locally as a fine talent. Immediately after graduation Mona headed off to acting school in the United States, and in 1929, at the age of twenty-eight, she arrived in New York City with dreams of making it big on Broadway.

What she found, however, were hundreds of others from across North America with the same ambitions. She managed to get a part as a chorus girl in a Ziegfeld Follies production, but soon came to realize that her chances at stardom were remote at best. To acquire skills that would support her she went to nursing school. Graduating with honours in 1935, she went to work in a Park Avenue doctor's office.

Her brother, in the meantime, had become a successful businessman who was frequently in New York and, one day in February 1937, he introduced Mona to his good friend Willem Leonhardt, a Dutch millionaire. It was love at first sight. After a whirlwind courtship the young couple left for Laren, Holland, where they were married on September 1, and where, after an around-the-world honeymoon, they settled into their grand mansion, "Ingleside." This was Mona's first marriage and Willem's second. He explained to her that his first marriage had ended in divorce after he discovered that his wife had given birth to another man's child. None of that mattered to Mona. She and Willem were madly in love and looking forward to a long and happy life together.

Willem's family didn't share in their happiness, however. This very confident, outspoken young Canadian was not the kind of woman they would have chosen for Willem.

Within months of the move into Ingleside, rumblings of war raced across Europe. Though Willem tried repeatedly to get Mona to return to Canada for her own safety, she refused to leave him. Once, he purchased a ticket on a steamship bound for Canada, and she promptly cashed it in and cancelled the booking. Mona knew her own mind and she was going nowhere.

The Nazi occupation of Holland began in May 1940, and in a matter of weeks, Mona, Willem, and several friends formed one of several resistance groups that sprang up across Holland. They decided that the best way they could contribute would be by helping downed allied airmen to hide from the Nazis and escape from the country.

Once they'd made the decision to resist the Nazis, they let go all their servants but one—Mona's personal maid. The fewer people who knew about the scheme, the better. And the now-empty servants' quarters on the top floor of Ingleside became accommodations for the airmen.

To ensure that unexpected visitors to the house did not catch sight of one of the airmen in the lower regions of the house, there would have to be an easily accessible hiding place.

As the master bedroom was the largest room, that would be the best location. Using the carpentry talents of some members of their resistance group, a wall, complete with a large closet, was constructed across one end of Mona and Willem's bedroom. At the back of the closet a secret door led to a hiding place where the men could wait until the all-clear signal was given.

A radio was hidden in the attic, and from there the resistance maintained contact with British forces. They had a network of supporters and a plan that would bring downed airmen to the house, then deliver them to safety. When the time was right, they would load the men into Willem's car—with forged papers in their pockets—and drive boldly past Nazi roadblocks to the coast, where fishing boats would carry them out to a waiting submarine. Together with their friends, Mona and Willem put their own lives at risk for more than a year, to save allied airmen.

Unfortunately, in late summer 1941, it became clear that there was a mole in their midst. One by one, Mona and Willem heard of the arrests of some group members and the execution of others. They knew it was only a matter of time before the Gestapo came pounding on their door. They mistakenly believed, however, that only Willem was in danger, and so, while he went into hiding, Mona stayed behind. On September 29, 1941, when the Gestapo came to Ingleside, she played the role of an innocent, naïve wife whose husband was away for a few days visiting relatives. The Nazis, however, knew otherwise. They arrested her on the spot, then took over their lovely home for use as a military headquarters.

A few months later, on December 21, they tracked down and arrested Willem, taking him to a separate prison. The next day, as her trial got underway, Mona had no idea her husband was in custody. The evidence was stacked against her, and not unexpectedly, she was found guilty and sentenced to death by firing squad. Drawing on her acting skills, Mona greeted the sentence with such composure that the judge approached her after the trial and said he would speak on her behalf. Sure enough, she was granted an appeal and a year later her sentence was commuted to life imprisonment at hard labour.

Mona was transported by cattle car from one prison to another over the next few years. At various times she was put to work on assembly lines, creating plywood wings for small aircraft, or assembling parts for bombs. At each prison, prisoners were treated with equal contempt by both male and female guards and Mona stood out, as she was the only Canadian. They were given limited food rations, were rarely allowed to wash, and large jars that sat in the corner of each four-person cell contained salt that they poured through their hair to kill lice. Women who became ill were sent to the infirmary, and were still required to work—knitting socks for German soldiers. Mona later told friends that she became adept at putting knots in the soles of the socks she made, in the hope that marching German soldiers would get blisters on their feet. It was her way of fighting back, if only in a small way.

In early 1945, she was moved by cattle car again, this time to the German town of Vechta, where there was an airfield, a train depot, and two prisons—one for men and one for women. The women continued to work twelve hour days. They were forbidden to talk to one another while they were working and collapsed with exhaustion into their beds at night. For most of Mona's imprisonment she shared a cell with three other women, and her bed consisted of a straw sack on an otherwise bare floor.

On March 24, they could hear planes approaching, and even though the anti-aircraft guns around the compound began firing, the planes kept coming. The sound of gunfire and bombs exploding was deafening and when the men's prison took a direct hit, killing all inside, the women began to panic. Some sought shelter deep in the women's prison building itself, while the warden ordered the gates thrown open so that others could take their chances outside. Dozens of women, including Mona and a young friend, a Dutch baroness, made a run for it. Behind them smoke billowed into the air, and Mona later told friends that she looked back only briefly and saw the bodies of women scattered across the field. At the insistence of her friend, the two women kept going.

They removed all clothing that would identify them as prisoners and buried it along the way, and the sweaters they wore were not much help in keeping out the cold as they traveled overland for the next three weeks, in the direction of the Dutch border. Along the way, they pretended to be refugees and stopped at farmhouses to beg or work for food. Where they could, they slept in barns. While Mona was fluent in German, she had a strong Canadian accent and they didn't want to draw any unwanted attention to themselves. So the baroness did all the talking, and Mona took on the role of her mentally disabled aunt, who had a speech impediment.

After travelling across 125 kilometres of Germany, the women were close to the Dutch border when they became separated after being given shelter by different farmers. So for the rest of the journey Mona continued on her own until she reached a small village near the border. As she walked down its main street, she was ecstatic to see that the British Army was now in control of the place.

She approached a group of young soldiers who were loading a truck, and she must have been a dreadful sight—emaciated and dishevelled, in ragged, dirty clothing, hobbling on blistered feet. The young men were wary of her, as they'd been warned that Nazis were using women to kill allied soldiers. She explained that she was a Canadian, from Nova Scotia, and that seemed to break the ice—at least it did with one young man, who said, *"I'm Clarence Leonard, and I'm from Halifax, and we are the North Nova Scotia Highlanders!"*

From there, things changed for Mona. Soon she was taken to a military hospital to have her infected feet taken care of and to get some nourishment. She weighed only eighty-seven pounds. Word of the arrival of this Canadian woman soon spread through the ranks, and, before much longer, she'd met up with several old friends from Wolfville—including Major General Harry Foster and Captains Richard Shaw, Vincent White, and Robbins Elliott.

Her friends took good care of her and soon had her back home safely at Ingleside, though it was a few months before Willem was able to join her. After being freed, he had been acting as a translator for the Americans.

Mona and Willem had a few happy years in their lovely house after the war, with Mona working tirelessly to restore the flower gardens that had been destroyed by the Nazi occupiers. But Willem never regained his strength, and died in 1956 as a result of the abuse he had suffered at the hands of the Nazis. Then Mona's life took a dramatic turn once again.

Within days of the funeral, Mona was shocked to learn that Willem's estate was to be divided between a mistress, his ex-wife, and the ex-wife's son, who, as it turned out, had been by Willem after all. For Mona, there was Ingleside, which she was forced to sell. In December 1957, devastated by the betrayal, Mona set sail for Nova Scotia.

When she arrived in Halifax and checked into the Lord Nelson Hotel, Mona began searching for a suitable apartment to rent. She found it in a large house at the corner of Inglis and Brussels Streets. Before long, Mona became a hit with her neighbours. A few of the ladies who lived in the building often held coffee parties for their friends from the neighbourhood, and soon Mona was joining them. They were absolutely enthralled by her and her experiences, although it was clear to them that Mona still carried the scars. Her apartment door was fitted with at least a half dozen deadbolts.

One of Mona's stories related to her first few months in Halifax. When walking along Barrington Street one morning, doing a bit of shopping, she looked up and saw a familiar face approaching. She stopped in her tracks. The man came right up to her, looked her straight in the eye but said nothing, then continued on his way. Mona was almost in a state of panic. She rushed home, locked her door behind her, and stayed there for several days. She told her friends about it later, explaining that she had just come face to face with one of her former guards.

Then one day, just by chance, Mona met an old friend. Major General Harry Foster was now retired, divorced, and living in Halifax. The two old friends began going for long walks together through the Public Gardens and in Point Pleasant Park, and before long a romance blossomed. In June 1959, Mona and Harry were married at the home of Harry's nephew on Young Avenue and eventually moved to Lobster Point, near Chester. For the first time in a long time, Mona was content. She loved Harry, and felt so very safe with him.

Sadly, five years later, she lost him to cancer and, in time, Mona moved back to Wolfville where she lived out the rest of her life. Mona died in 1976, and is buried in the Willowbank Cemetery. Her stone reads simply:

Mona L. Parsons
1901–1976
Wife of
Major General H. W. Foster,
C.B.E. and D.S.O.

Though Mona received commendations from both United States General Dwight D. Eisenhower and British Air Chief Marshal Sir Arthur Tedder for her heroic efforts in aiding allied airmen during the Second World War, few Nova Scotians are aware of her sacrifice.

26

SINGALONG WITH WINNIE

(1943 and 1944)

A great man leaves an indelible impression.

It was September 14, 1943. The world had been at war for four years and today Halifax was expecting the most famous man in the Empire to drop by. At the train station, as a military guard stood respectfully to one side, Mayor John Lloyd and his staff waited anxiously for the arrival of Winston Churchill.

Churchill was on his way from Quebec City where he'd been meeting with Prime Minister Mackenzie King and U.S. President Roosevelt. From Halifax, he would be taken back to Britain in a convoy of Royal Navy warships.

The moment, and Churchill, finally arrived, and once the formalities had been taken care of, the prime minister and the mayor, with a collection of security guards following close behind, set off on a tour of the city. They stopped at the Public Gardens where Churchill got out of the car to stretch his legs and, against the advice of his security detail, began wandering along the paths, chatting amiably with awestruck Haligonians. He exasperated the guards even further when he headed for the gates and, with Major

Lloyd beaming beside him, took a stroll along Spring Garden Road, stopping frequently to speak with people along the way.

Halifax had been playing a major role in the war and Churchill acknowledged as much in his conversations with locals. He made sure to express, to everyone he met, the deep gratitude of the British people and other allied nations for the sacrifices Haligonians had been making. Not only were many of their own sons, brothers, and fathers off fighting, but in Halifax convoys were being equipped with much-needed supplies for Britain, and young men from across Canada were being deployed to the battlefields of Europe. And Haligonians were all too aware of the battles raging on the Atlantic, as the sound of gunfire could often be heard on downtown streets.

So that he could get the best view the city had to offer, Mayor Lloyd then took Mr. Churchill to Citadel Hill, where a platform had been erected at the ramparts. From there, they looked out over the entire expanse of the city and the harbour, and saw the British warships that were standing by to take Churchill back to London.

Churchill turned to Lloyd and said, *"Now, sir, we know that your city is much more than a shed on a wharf."*

Soldiers at the Citadel were thrilled to shake his hand, and all along the streets hundreds of war-weary people were waving small Union Jack flags, as a sign of respect for a man they considered a hero. At the dock, where Mayor Lloyd was joined by a delegation of politicians to see Churchill off, there were a few speeches and a lot of cheers from a large nearby crowd.

A year later, Roosevelt, Mackenzie King, and Churchill were preparing for the second Quebec Conference and increasingly optimistic that this could be the last meeting of its kind. It appeared the war was drawing to a successful conclusion.

At Halifax, with tugboats leading the way, the sight of the *Queen Mary* steaming into the harbour on September 10 dramatically lifted the spirits of those who saw it. It was the first time the great liner had been in port since the war began, and most took that as a very positive sign. A short time after it berthed, crowds of passengers left the ship to do an hour or two of sightseeing before their journey to New York resumed.

No one seemed to pay much attention to three dark blue sedans parked nearby.

When things quieted down a bit, a heavy-set man brandishing a large cigar, in the company of a woman and several naval officers, left the ship and walked toward the waiting automobiles. Winston Churchill and his wife Clementine were setting off on the second leg of their journey to Quebec, and time was of the essence. The cars headed straight for the train station.

However, as they had been since the beginning of the war, Halifax streets were teeming with young men from every service, and there wasn't one who wouldn't recognize Winston Churchill when he saw him. The small caravan of cars had barely set out when it passed several young men on a street corner. They couldn't believe their eyes! Winston Churchill was in town! They wasted no time spreading the word, and as the official caravan was pulling up in front of the train station entrance, hordes of young men were rushing along Barrington Street and down Inglis Street in its direction.

Churchill and Clementine were escorted quickly through the station and onto the platform where a train with a reserved car was waiting. The security forces closed ranks around them, and barred the platform doors. They were used to guarding dignitaries, but none as popular as Churchill; they knew that if they let anything happen to him their lives wouldn't be worth living. Hundreds of sailors, soldiers, and airmen converged on the place only to come up against the locked platform doors and several armed guards.

Churchill heard the commotion and looked out of the train to see what was happening. When he did, he stepped onto the platform and told the guards to withdraw their weapons and open the doors. The young men, who had been behaving rather boisterously before the doors were opened, suddenly became very quiet in the presence of the great man himself. Churchill greeted them warmly and spoke to them candidly and from the heart about how much he personally appreciated the sacrifices they and their families were making.

And just when it seemed the emotion might be a bit much, he mentioned some of his favourite wartime songs and asked the crowd to join him in singing *"When the Lights Come on Again."* For the next half hour, Churchill and these hundreds of young lads continued singing. *"It's a Long Way to Tipperary,"* *"We'll Meet Again,"* *"Pack up Your Troubles,"* and *"Keep the Home Fires Burning."* Clementine joined them for the last song, a rousing rendition of *"O Canada."*

When it was time to leave, hundreds of pairs of hands waved goodbye. Memories of their singalong with Winnie would stay with the men forever.

The bronze statue of Churchill that stands on the grounds of the Halifax Memorial Library on Spring Garden Road was created by the noted sculptor Oscar Nemon, from a photograph taken of Churchill in 1943, when he took that stroll along Spring Garden Road.

27

CHRISTMAS AT SEA

(1944)

Bringing joy to refugee children.

During the Second World War, people in both Halifax and Sydney, Nova Scotia, became familiar with the sight of convoys of merchant ships marshalling before heading out into the dangerous North Atlantic under the protection of allied warships. These convoys made an enormous contribution to the war effort by bringing much-needed supplies to Britain and beyond.

In mid-December 1944, in a convoy leaving Britain for a return voyage to North America, one of the merchant ships was carrying an extra-special cargo. On board were the wives and children of Canadian soldiers, along with refugees from France, Czechoslovakia, and a dozen other war-torn countries.

As they would be spending Christmas in the mid-Atlantic, the captain and crew had taken up a collection and, before their departure from Liverpool, had purchased toys and candy for the dozens of children aboard. Unfortunately, Christmas trees were a rare commodity at the time and they weren't able to find one of those, but the cook would prepare a special breakfast on

Christmas morning, and the toys and candies would be distributed at that time.

They were well out to sea on Christmas Eve afternoon when a Canadian warship pulled out of the outer escort and came alongside the merchant ship. The captain read the frigate's signal light from the bridge, which blinked out: *"We're putting a line aboard."* Later, the captain admitted, *"I thought it was a message from the convoy commodore giving me the devil for something."*

A line was fired across the bow, and two members of the crew rushed to attach it to their vessel. The sound drew passengers nervously to the deck. After the experiences of the previous few years, loud noises made them anxious, but they soon found there was nothing to fear. All along the rail, men, women, and children watched in awe as a ten-foot Christmas tree was winched across the fifty-foot gap between the ships.

Before it reached them, Canadian servicemen gathered on the deck of the frigate and, as loudly as they could, belted out a selection of Christmas carols. When the tree hit the deck every man, woman, and child on that ship—including the war-weary crew—instantly got the Christmas spirit! To most of the children, a Christmas tree was something they had heard about, but never experienced. At the sight of the little ones jumping up and down with joy, the frigate's crew burst into laughter. After the war, they told their families that bringing that afternoon of joy to a bunch of children who'd been through so much was as rewarding to them as it was to the passengers on the ship.

After the ship landed, the story spread, and several newspapers including the *Toronto Star* interviewed the crew and related this heartwarming Christmas story through their eyes.

Two men took the tree down to the dining hall and set it up. The cook, filled with more energy than he'd had in a long while, headed straight for the galley and found just enough ingredients to make a fine cake. Meanwhile, passengers and crew alike headed for their cabins to find ribbons, trinkets, and decorations of all sorts to trim the tree, as well as a few treasures to bestow as gifts. The captain remarked that both he and the crew were behaving like a bunch of kids themselves.

After a visit to the dispensary, one merchant marine officer headed to his cabin and for several hours was busy on a special project of his own. He took a jacket with red lining and turned it inside out, and, with a large roll of cotton batting, trimmed its cuffs and collars in white, then did the same to a stocking cap. There was just enough cotton left over to make himself a full, white beard.

That evening, passengers and crew alike gathered in the dining hall, happily singing carols, decorating the tree, and eating freshly-baked cake. When the tree was finally trimmed to everyone's satisfaction, a young Irish nurse pulled up a stool and told some of her favourite Christmas stories to the wide-eyed children gathered around her.

Suddenly, the little ones were startled by the sound of a deep belly laugh, *"Ho...ho...ho!"* coming from the doorway, and much to their absolute delight, the appearance of Santa Claus himself! With the assistance of the crew, who'd filled a large bag with the toys and trinkets they'd purchased in port, Santa made a very special day even better.

The captain commented it had been *"the most thrilling thing I have seen in my thirty-one years at sea,"* and that the gift of a Christmas tree by Canadian servicemen had been a *"most wonderful gesture"* that had brought such joy to so many people that it was, without doubt, a Christmas to remember.

28

WANDERING SPIRITS

(1746–2012)

Just what is lurking in the dark recesses of Halifax?

Over several generations of Haligonians, there have been those who claim to have seen, at the break of day, the spirit of an Indian warrior sprinting across the slope of the Citadel before fading into the growing light. Others are adamant that, as the modern city of Halifax begins a new day, long-dead souls, after roaming its old streets and lanes during the darkest hours, slip out of sight once again.

Halifax's ghostly encounters go back to its very beginning, when settlers began noticing and following the spirit of the duc d'Anville as he walked into the water near his grave site on Georges Island and across to the town, then made his way along the shoreline to a beach on the Bedford Basin. There, the ghost was seen walking directly into the water, presumably looking for his lost men and ships. After a disastrous crossing from France, hundreds of d'Anville's men had died of typhus in a makeshift hospital on that beach and before the rest of the fleet returned to France, five of his ships had been scuttled in that harbour to prevent them falling into British hands. Folks living along the shore claimed that on the nights that d'Anville walked, they could hear invisible ships creaking, their sails flapping in the breeze. There were so many sightings over a hundred and fifty years, in fact, that in the late nineteenth century the government commissioned a scientific study into the matter. No satisfactory explanation was ever found.

Many Haligonians, particularly those who live in Victorian houses in the older part of the city, easily accept reports of ghostly sightings, because they, too, have had their own strange experiences—doors that open and close by themselves, the creaking of staircase steps when no one is there, or the sound of footsteps pacing an empty hallway.

In the years after the War of 1812, soldiers and civilians alike reported the nightly appearance of a distraught young woman with babe in arms, walking along the perimeter of the Ordinance Yard's stone wall in the direction of the harbour. At the end of a wharf, the pair would quietly slip over the edge and into the water. Repeatedly, the constables had been called to the scene to find only distressed people who had been unable to stop her. Street urchins knew her tale and, for a penny, were happy to relate that she was the abandoned lover of a heartless soldier who worked on the other side of the wall, at the Ordinance Yard. Each night, the girl would cry for help at the iron gates, before she began her desperate walk. The nightly visits unnerved the soldier's friends, so the story goes, and though he pretended not to be alarmed, he repeatedly requested a transfer to another station. When the transfer was finally granted, the heartless soldier gladly boarded a ship and left Halifax and his troubles behind. Or so he thought. Witnesses noticed, as his ship sailed out of the harbour, that standing on the deck was a weeping young woman with a babe in her arms. That ghost was never seen in Halifax again.

As if the story of the mother and babe were not enough to stir the imaginations of Haligonians, the topic of conversation in the city's finest drawing rooms, and in its taverns and brothels on the grim streets east of the Citadel, soon turned to the repeated sightings of another apparition.

At dusk each evening over a period of several months, a man dressed in civilian clothes and—according to eyewitness reports—standing from twelve to sixteen feet in height, appeared near the barracks on the slope of the Citadel (about the site of the present police station) and made his way down Buckingham Street toward the dockyard, where he lit his pipe from a lamppost and rested his arms upon the top of the Ordinance Yard wall. Soldiers on the other side were taken aback by the appearance of this enormous fellow who was able to lean comfortably over the ten-foot wall. Again the police were called out. This time they set up a patrol along Buckingham Street to wait for the ghost to appear and when he did, the chase began. For his size, the huge fellow was light of foot and ran easily down the hill until he reached a building at the corner of Water Street that had an open window and, despite its being much smaller than he and unlikely to accommodate his large form, the ghost slipped easily through it and simply disappeared. That was the last anyone ever saw of him.

In 1876, the entire town was caught up once again in the story of a haunting—this time in a bakery near Cornwallis Street. Though its previous owner had died two years earlier, it seemed his spirit was either unable or unwilling to move on. From the day that the new baker and his family moved in, they were not allowed a moment's peace. The ghost would make his presence known at all hours by loudly stomping around the shop and attached house, rattling windows, and opening and slamming doors. The family was understandably frightened and, to put a stop to their ordeal, the new baker enlisted the help of friends, neighbours, and a parish priest.

On New Year's Eve 1876, they purposely double-barred and bolted one of the doors the ghost commonly used and held vigil well into the night. Shortly after midnight, they heard the sound of heavy footsteps approaching. Suddenly, the bolted door began to shake violently as though unseen hands were attacking it in a rage and, as the terrified onlookers remained crouched in a corner of the shop, the attack continued until the entire shop, its contents, and the adjacent house shook and trembled. In the days that followed, the baker pleaded for the support and advice of anyone who might be able to suggest what to do. What, he asked, could be making the former baker so angry that he would not leave his old shop? A suggestion by an old fellow who lived nearby that the former baker might have been upset by the removal of a favourite stove from his kitchen was dismissed—then later reconsidered. Willing to try anything, the baker retrieved the old stove from where it had been discarded and returned it to the kitchen. Almost immediately, his torment came to an end.

The town's naval history has also had a ghostly impact. After a battle off Boston Harbour on June 1, 1813, during the War of 1812, the small British ship HMS *Shannon* was victorious over the much larger American vessel, USS *Chesapeake*. Later, as the *Shannon* led the captured *Chesapeake* triumphantly into Halifax Harbour, cheering crowds watched from the shore while military bands played "Rule Britannia." Since then, on quiet nights when fog has settled over the harbour, some claim to have seen the *Shannon* again sail into the harbour with the *Chesapeake* close behind, blood and gore running from her decks as though the battle had just happened, rather than having taken place so many lifetimes ago.

And on Black Rock Beach at Point Pleasant Park, some hear the sound of metal gibbets and their gruesome load rattling in the night breeze and feel that the lost souls who perished there are still tied to that shore.

To this very day, there are many "haunted houses" in Halifax, some well known, some not. There's the old house on Robie Street near Jubilee Road where the glass of a window, regardless of how many times it was changed, turned black overnight and, though several all-night vigils were held to get to the bottom of the mystery, no one was ever able to prevent or explain it. Then, there's the house on Barrington Street near Bishop where the building's modern occupants have been startled by the sounds of crying babies, possibly because that house stands at the site of the town's first orphanage, built in 1750. In a house on Morris Street an empty rocking chair rocks repeatedly, without the slightest human touch. In a house on Fenwick Street an antique radio turns itself on and off; and in a house overlooking the Bedford Basin a small child saw her late grandfather sitting in his favourite chair.

For believers, the spirits of its past continue to roam the lanes and streets of old Halifax, and if you aren't quite so easily convinced, why not take the time to consider…the next time the floorboards creak or a door swings open or you feel a sudden draft…is it really because your house is old, settling, and in need of insulation? Or is it something else?